An ATLAS of
THE ENGLISH LAKES

PICTORIAL CHARTS
compiled from
an Exploration of the Shorelines of the
LAKE DISTRICT
On Foot and by Canoe

Devised, surveyed and drawn by John Wilson Parker

THE SEVENTEEN LAKES

LISTED IN ORDER OF THEIR APPEARANCE IN THIS BOOK

1 **WINDERMERE**
2 GRASMERE
3 RYDAL WATER
4 ELTER WATER
5 ESTHWAITE WATER
6 **CONISTON WATER**

7 WAST WATER
8 ENNERDALE WATER
9 LOWES WATER
10 CRUMMOCK WATER
11 BUTTERMERE

12 BASSENTHWAITE LAKE
13 **DERWENT WATER**
14 THIRLMERE RESERVOIR
15 BROTHERS WATER
16 **ULLSWATER**
17 HAWESWATER RESERVOIR

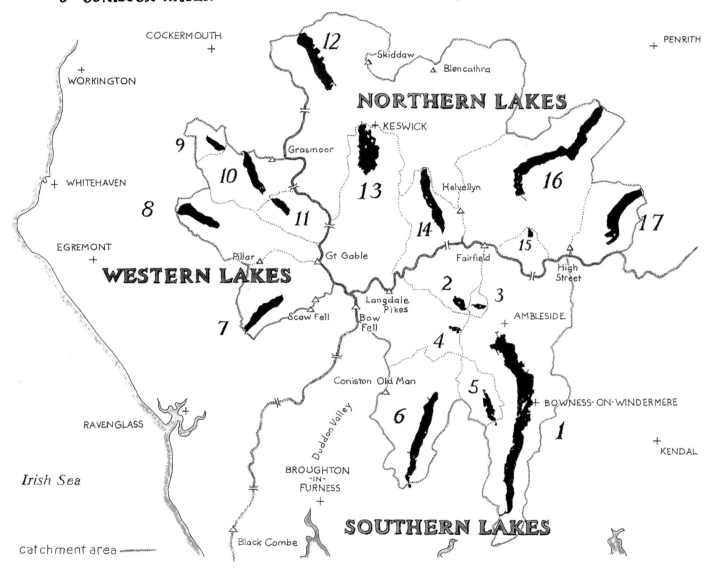

DIAGRAMS and CHART INDICES of each **GROUP** accompany the INTRODUCTIONS:

	Southern Lakes	Western Lakes	Northern Lakes
"Around the Shores"	page 6	page 8	page 9
"On the Water"	10	12	14
"The Charts"	16	18	20
Notes and Remarks	22-23, 36	51, 54	60 61, 77-78

An ATLAS of
THE ENGLISH LAKES

PICTORIAL CHARTS
compiled from
an Exploration of the Shorelines of the
LAKE DISTRICT
On Foot and by Canoe

Devised, surveyed and drawn by John Wilson Parker

CICERONE

2 POLICE SQUARE, MILNTHORPE, CUMBRIA, LA7 7PY
www.cicerone.co.uk

This work is dedicated to all –

Benefactors, Landowners,

Proprietors and Workers,

Professionals or Volunteers,

who maintain the landscape

and conserve the ecology

of

England's Most Beautiful Corner.

The author wishes to record his appreciation of
the support, encouragement and suggestions given by his Wife, Family and Close Friends.

Wardens, Rangers, Proprietors and Staff of
the official authorities and private establishments which he approached
contributed with useful information and advice.
Their willing co-operation is acknowledged with gratitude.

PROLOGUE

THE GREATEST books about the Outdoors, the truly inspiring ones, decline to list, classify or quantify the places they describe. Instead they recreate the spiritual feelings and physical sensations that nature evokes and imposes, sharing rewards or lessons gained from experiences and personal exploration. One home example, John Wyatt's *The Shining Levels*, contains few place names and mentions no "must-see" locations.

This book is opposite in character. Like Wainwright's Fell Guides, it is the result of an objective exploration which has broadened my own horizons. Living on its fringe and being paid to revise or re-survey the Ordnance Survey plans - alongside fell-walking, climbing, rescuing and skiing in my spare time - encouraged a belief that I knew the Lake District well. But Windermere, Coniston Water and Derwent Water had been ignored too often during early morning flights to the crags and summits of the fells.

When early retirement broke a nine-year exile my wife, Jenny, encouraged our acquisition of a Canadian canoe on our re-establishment in Cumbria. The querying of the possibilities of following the shorelines of each lake in the Pathfinder, allied to a lifetime's habit of map-making and map-reading, inevitably led me into this pleasurable, self-imposed task.

The joy of discovery, previously enacted among the fells and mountains, was re-born. A new dimension had been found. Physical output in a parallel branch of outdoor adventure might be rewarded in a similar fashion.

During our exploratory work in the light canoe we found we were quite able, under our own steam, to attain the furthest reaches of the lakes from available put-ins. Those trips constitute relaxing half-day excursions. With training, the entire shoreline of any lake could be traced during a full day, although Windermere and its islands might prove more than a marathon. Nevertheless the end-to-end (Fell Foot to Waterhead) traverse of this, the longest lake, is a highly recommended day's paddle.

Gliding on mirrored calms through mists gilded by early or late sunglow gave greatest satisfaction. The Indian Stroke (a sculling action) propels a Canadian canoe gently, silently to more intimate sights and sounds of nature and wildlife than those experienced on foot or other means of transport.

Several lake walking circuits are well established and justifiably popular. Fell-walkers use them for off-day activity, but classic viewpoints of the Cumbrian mountains are often positioned on, or just above, lake shores and are best appreciated in decent visibility. A greater variety of terrain and wildlife will be encountered than on many an upland walk. Promenades with shops, steamer piers, formal gardens, green pastures, reedbeds, marsh, woodland, shingle bays, precipitous rocks and wildfowl will entertain on these tours which range from endurance tests to leisurely rambles.

Born in Middlesex, John Parker spent his school-days in Blackpool. Solace was found cycling to the Lakes and Dales, then touring and racing with the Cleveleys Road Club. He left school to join the Ordnance Survey in 1957. After National Service he adopted his wife's passion for fell-walking and moved to Westmorland, where he took up rock-climbing and mountaineering. Since retirement Jenny and he have lived in Grange-over-Sands.

First Published 2002
Reprinted 2004

ISBN   1 85284 355 1

The Charts in this book are based on Ordnance Survey 1:10,560 & 1:10,000 mapping
Crown Copyright Reserved

Other Cicerone books by the same author:
Scrambles in Skye

Publisher:

Cicerone Press
2 Police Square
MILNTHORPE
Cumbria
England
LA7 7PY

Tel 015395 62069
Fax 015395 63417

www.cicerone.co.uk
Email: info@cicerone.co.uk

Front cover: Derwent Water from Castle Head

4

CONTENTS

AROUND THE SHORES   SOUTHERN LAKES

Distances indicate complete walking circuits and include "culs-de-sac"

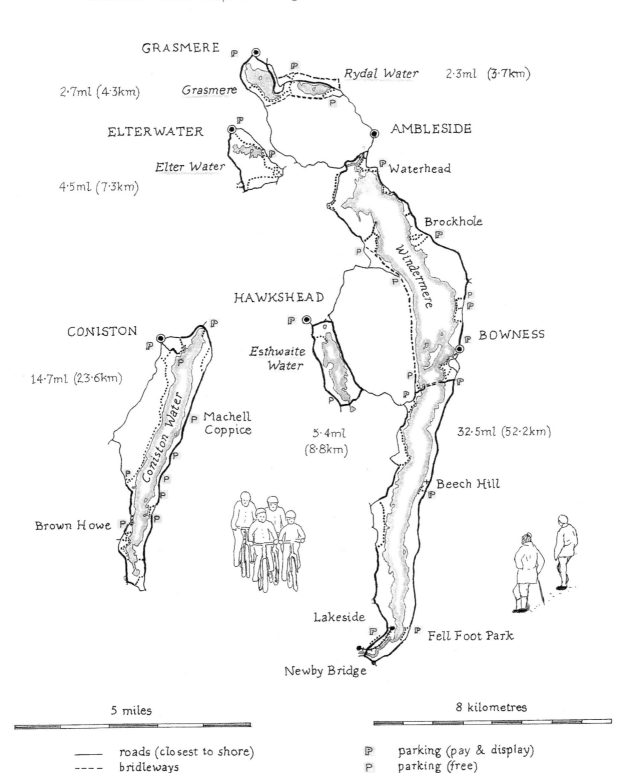

GRASMERE

Rydal Water   2·3ml (3·7km)

2·7ml (4·3km)   Grasmere

ELTERWATER   AMBLESIDE

Elter Water   Waterhead

4·5ml (7·3km)   Brockhole

Windermere

HAWKSHEAD

CONISTON   BOWNESS

Esthwaite Water

14·7ml (23·6km)

Machell Coppice

Coniston Water   5·4ml (8·8km)   32·5ml (52·2km)

Beech Hill

Brown Howe

Lakeside   Fell Foot Park

Newby Bridge

5 miles   8 kilometres

——— roads (closest to shore)   P parking (pay & display)
- - - - bridleways   P parking (free)
.... paths (featured on Charts)   ◉ VILLAGE (shops, catering)
+++++ railway

AROUND THE SHORES

AIMED primarily at canoeists and kayakers, this survey will hopefully cater for all those interested in exploring the shorelines of the English Lakes be they on foot or afloat, in the saddle or armchair bound.

Important features of the Charts are the routes which take the reader on walks which pursue lake shorelines as closely as proprietorial rights allow. Indeed, only rights-of-way on FOOT follow extensive sections of **Elter Water, Wast Water, Ennerdale Water, Brothers Water** and **Haweswater Reservoir.** RAMBLERS will have no difficulty in using them. "Townies" will find, however, that Lake District "paths" include: very steep climbs and descents, steep and smooth rocks, rough and loose stones, wet or boggy stretches. The wearing of lightweight fell-walking boots and careful footwork dispel injury or discomfort. Seasoned visitors to the area assume it will rain before the walk is completed and carry the means to prevent getting soaked or chilled.

RIDERS of HORSES and CYCLES require the Ordnance Survey maps recommended on page 15. Lakes which have a complete circuit of road and bridle/cycle ways offer rewarding and enjoyable excursions. Quiet lanes and tracks are the most pleasant means of visiting the western shores of **Windermere.** One tour of **Ullswater** could involve crossing Boredale Hause, a classic objective for "rough-stuff" cycle-tourists and mountain-bikers. **Esthwaite Water, Coniston Water, Bassenthwaite Lake, Derwent Water** and **Thirlmere Reservoir** can all be pedalled round by ROAD. Apart from **Ullswater** and **Windermere** other lakes circumnavigable by road and BRIDLEWAY are: **Grasmere** with **Rydal Water, Lowes Water** and **Buttermere.**

A burgeoning and welcome number of MINI-BUS services catering for tourists and ramblers are operated by the likes of the National Trust. Information offices supply time-tables and details for these as well as the REGULAR BUS ROUTES which serve communities along lake shores. An amalgam of authorities publish a general time-table/guide for boat; train- and bus-users in and around the county, entitled *Getting Around Cumbria.* Copies should be available from information offices (see appendix). Public transport may be convenient for car-users wishing to link the ends of linear walks. Motor cars or vans are useful for conveying canoes, cycles and other gear or supplies to the scene of outdoor activities.

Paths and other routes depicted on the Charts appeared to be open to the public at the time they were investigated. However the author cannot guarantee their status as rights-of-way. Readers should be prepared to observe any restrictions in force on the hour or day of their visit.

Several WHEELCHAIR-friendly routes with facilities for the disabled exist within the National Park. The Authority's booklet *Countryside Access for People with Limited Mobility* includes established sections of pathways at: Cockshott Point, Claife shore and Red Nab (**Windermere CHARTS V-s, V-s/N** and **VI-w**); White Moss (**Grasmere** and **Rydal Water**); The Boating Centre and Water Head (**Coniston Water IV**); Maggie's Bridge (**Lowes Water**); a circuit of Cockshot Wood and Friar's Crag (**Derwent Water I-N/S**). Shorter "pushes" are listed by other lakes and within parks, gardens and the grounds of houses open to visitors. Note that gateways and surfaced paths appear on the Charts.

FISHERMEN require undisturbed calm. Noise or intrusion may ruin the point of their acquiring a licence, equipment, expertise and patience. Respect their space. Canoeists should (please) give them a wide berth. A cast line can extend a good way from shore. Anyone fancying a day out with rod and line will find no more inspiring places for this pastime than Cumbria. Laurence Tetley's *Guide* (see appendix) comprehensively describes and details local licensing regulations, available locations - on both still and running water, plus tackle shops and local associations.

Please remember and observe the COUNTRY CODE. Guard against all risk of fire. Fasten gates. Keep dogs under proper control. Stay on the paths across farm land. Avoid damaging fences, hedges and walls. Leave no litter. Safeguard water supplies. Protect wild life, plants and trees. Respect the life of the countryside. And go carefully on country roads.

AROUND THE SHORES   WESTERN LAKES

Distances indicate complete walking circuits and include "culs-de-sac"

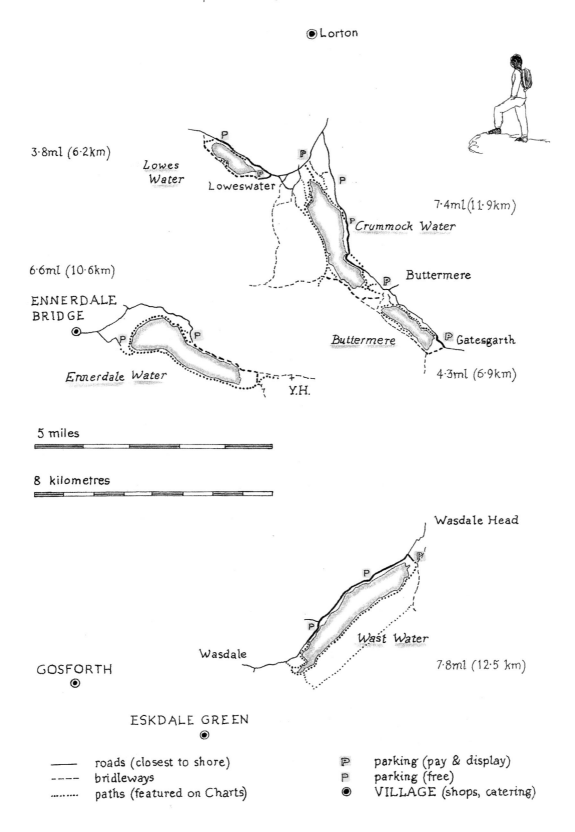

⦿ Lorton

3·8ml (6·2km)

Lowes Water

Loweswater

Crummock Water

7·4ml (11·9km)

Buttermere

6·6ml (10·6km)

ENNERDALE
BRIDGE
⦿

Ennerdale Water

Buttermere

Gatesgarth

4·3ml (6·9km)

Y.H.

5 miles

8 kilometres

Wasdale Head

Wasdale

Wast Water

GOSFORTH
⦿

7·8ml (12·5 km)

ESKDALE GREEN
⦿

———— roads (closest to shore)
- - - - bridleways
········ paths (featured on Charts)

P parking (pay & display)
P parking (free)
⦿ VILLAGE (shops, catering)

AROUND THE SHORES

NORTHERN LAKES

Distances indicate complete walking circuits and include "culs-de-sac"

🅿 parking (pay & display)
🅿 parking (free)
◉ VILLAGE (shops, catering)

——— roads (closest to shore)
– – – bridleways
········· paths (featured on Charts)

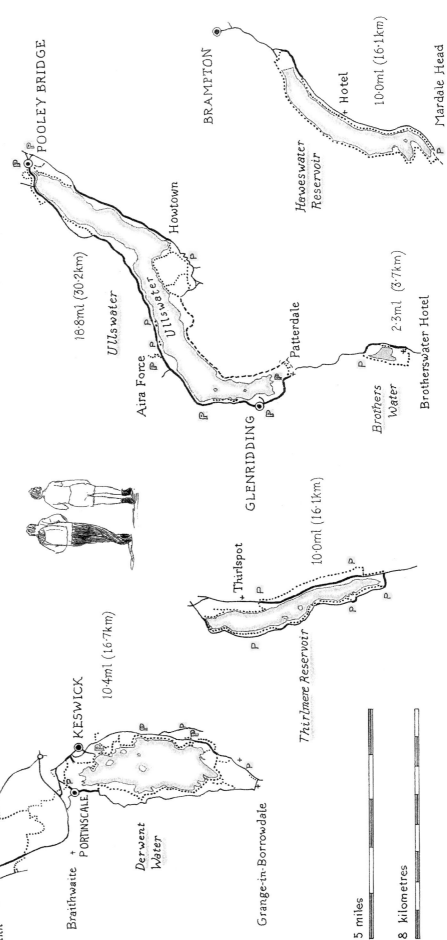

Ouse Bridge

Bassenthwaite Lake

15.5ml (24.9km)

Dodd Wood

Pheasant Inn

Braithwaite

PORTINSCALE

KESWICK

10.4ml (16.7km)

Derwent Water

Grange-in-Borrowdale

Thirlspot

Thirlmere Reservoir

10.0ml (16.1km)

GLENRIDDING

Brothers Water

2.3ml (3.7km)

Brotherswater Hotel

Aira Force

Ullswater

Ullswater

18.8ml (30.2km)

Howtown

Patterdale

POOLEY BRIDGE

BRAMPTON

Haweswater Reservoir

+ Hotel

10.0ml (16.1km)

Mardale Head

5 miles

8 kilometres

9

ON THE WATER

SOUTHERN LAKES

Distances indicate maximum inshore circuits and include round-island detours

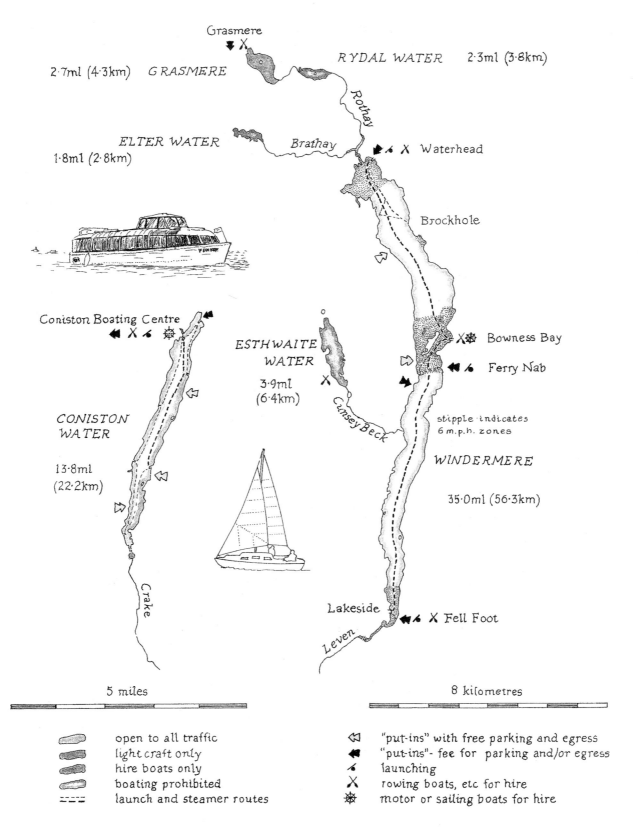

Grasmere

RYDAL WATER   2·3ml (3·8km)

2·7ml (4·3km)   GRASMERE

Rothay

ELTER WATER   Brathay

1·8ml (2·8km)   Waterhead

Brockhole

Coniston Boating Centre

ESTHWAITE
WATER
3·9ml
(6·4km)

X Bowness Bay

Ferry Nab

CONISTON
WATER

13·8ml
(22·2km)

Cumsey Beck

stipple indicates
6 m.p.h. zones

WINDERMERE

35·0ml (56·3km)

Crake

Lakeside   X Fell Foot

Leven

5 miles   8 kilometres

	open to all traffic
	light craft only
	hire boats only
	boating prohibited
- - -	launch and steamer routes

	"put-ins" with free parking and egress
	"put-ins"- fee for parking and/or egress
	launching
X	rowing boats, etc for hire
✳	motor or sailing boats for hire

ON THE WATER

The famed STEAMER SERVICES deserve everyone's patronage. For the fit, elderly and disabled alike they provide the most appropriate means of transport for viewing the magnificent landscapes. Ramblers might enrich a linear walk by taking advantage of these vessels which add such grace to the natural scenery. **Windermere** loses an element of its character whenever the *SWAN, TEAL* and *TERN* are out of commission during the off-season. Similarly the *RAVEN* and *LADY OF THE LAKE* enhance **Ullswater,** while **Coniston Water**'s appeal has been strengthened by the restoration of the *GONDOLA*. Other cruisers and launches serve as public transport on these lakes and **Derwent Water**. The prosaic but most patronised of all these services is the Windermere Ferry which, throughout the year, carries vehicles as well as passengers across the lake between Bowness and Hawkshead.

POWER BOAT enthusiasts have a chance to let off steam on **Windermere** during one mid-week, out-of-season period when trials are run and attempts made on World Records. This traditional event spans a century of injury-free dedication to speed!

Travelling under SAIL must be the most sporting and absorbing method of getting about on water anywhere. Rapid progress before a stiff breeze would render these Charts a little unwieldy. Perhaps a "passenger" could follow progress with them in calm conditions. Sailing CLUBS operate on **Windermere, Coniston, Bassenthwaite Lake, Derwent Water** and **Ullswater.**

During the milder season cruisers, more appropriate to the Riviera or Caribbean, are often seen taking their owners the length of **Windermere**. Their passing will be marked by the ensuing wash rocking everyone else's craft and eroding the shore's vegetation. Anyone can hire more appropriately powered MOTOR BOATS on **Windermere, Coniston Water, Derwent Water** and **Ullswater** to enjoy a relaxing hour or two with their friends and families. Ecologically-minded operators have introduced electrically-powered models to these lakes. Private motor-powered boats must be registered at the Lake Warden's office at Ferry Nab or the information centres at Bowness and Waterhead before they may be used on **Windermere**. Water- and jet-skiing on this lake will hardly be feasible when the TEN MPH SPEED LIMIT - already in force on Coniston, Derwent and Ullswater and set by a very expensive and drawn-out public enquiry held in 1994 - is imposed. No doubt the measure will lure even greater numbers of peace-seeking visitors and lake-users which natural beauty attracts. In the meantime avoid de-restricted areas during weekends and holiday periods.

Nevertheless ROWING remains the most popular form of boat hire on the "big four". **Grasmere, Crummock Water** and **Buttermere** also offer this facility, which is the only way to explore two other small lakes - **Esthwaite Water** and **Lowes Water.**

CANOES, KAYAKS and SAILBOARDS are easily transportable and, like sailing dinghies, are usually brought to the shore whenever and wherever their owners fancy a day out on the water. Several boating centres on the popular lakes hire canoes, kayaks and sailing boats, offering a splendid opportunity to test one's compatibility and skill without the commitment of purchasing a "white elephant". To protect the ecology the National Trust have chosen to BAN boating on **Rydal Water, Elter Water** and **Brothers Water.** Happily **Grasmere, Wast Water, Crummock Water** and **Buttermere** are available for NON-MOTORISED craft but numbers are restricted on a daily basis. North West Water permits wind- and muscle-powered boats on **Ennerdale Water** and **Thirlmere Reservoir,** but **Haweswater Reservoir** remains a no-row/sail/paddle area. Please avoid backwaters and reedbeds on any lake, where WILDLIFE seek refuge and nesting birds need undisturbed quiet.

SWIMMING is the most natural way of moving on or in water. For the unwary it is hazardous. See the safety notes below.

Thanks to global-warming, SKATING is practically obsolete. Real Winter conditions last invaded The Lakes during 1963. Do not be tempted onto any ice until oxen have been thoroughly roasted, fires extinguished and the thermometer remains well below freezing. Even in such conditions underwater springs will create weak patches in the ice!

Distances indicate maximum inshore circuits and include round-island detours

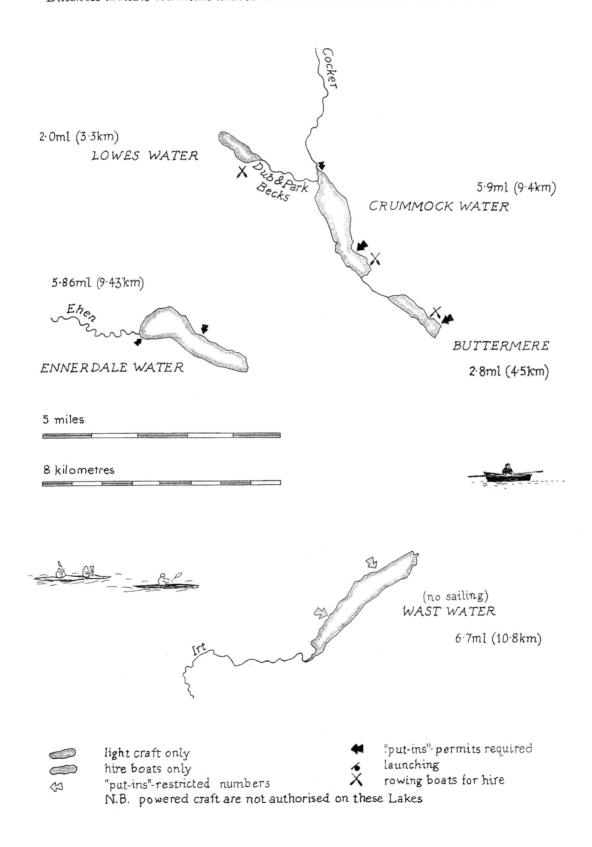

2·0ml (3·3km)
LOWES WATER

Cocker

Dub & Park Becks

5·9ml (9·4km)
CRUMMOCK WATER

5·86ml (9·43km)

Ehen

ENNERDALE WATER

BUTTERMERE
2·8ml (4·5km)

5 miles

8 kilometres

(no sailing)
WAST WATER
6·7ml (10·8km)

Irt

light craft only
hire boats only
"put-ins"-restricted numbers

"put-ins"-permits required
launching
rowing boats for hire

N.B. powered craft are not authorised on these Lakes

SAFETY and WEATHER

THE SAFE USE of waterborne craft is ultimately the responsibility of those in their charge. You should make it your business to read and understand any safety codes for the watersports in which you are involved. There are stringent rules and procedures for sailors and drivers of motorised craft to observe and follow. To make life easier for them and safer for everyone, light craft should avoid busy shipping lanes and keep to the shallows whenever possible. Heading a small boat into the bow-waves of passing cruisers or speedboats minimises the risk of being swamped or overturned. Passenger craft have full priority over any other boats on their approach to piers and jetties.

In an emergency, alert the Rescue Services by dialling 999.

The provision of TECHNICAL ADVICE is not an aim of this book. Qualified instruction is available in the Lake District and elsewhere. Several recommended books include *Path of the Paddle* (Key Porter Books, Toronto, 1988) by the late Bill Mason of Canada, a classic tome for the Canadian canoe. *The Outward Bound Canoeing Handbook* (see appendix) covers all aspects of canoeing and kayaking in Britain.

While LAUNCHING your craft take care that you do not inconvenience, injure or damage others or their property. Leave vehicles in a safe position where they will not obstruct traffic or farming activities. The correct size BUOYANCY AID must be worn and adjusted for safety by every member of the crew as they go aboard. Their ability to swim whilst wearing sailing/canoeing gear and clothing is of paramount importance.

Take heed of the prevailing or forecast WEATHER. The National Park Rangers provide an informative "Weatherline Service" (tel 017687 75757). Tailored for fell-goers, it can prove useful for sailors too. Strong WINDS cause real danger. Any waters in mountain country are subject to sudden squalls or downdraughts. The sight of yachts with well-filled spinnakers approaching each other is not too unusual on Windermere or Ullswater. A moderate wind builds up very large waves at the end of long, open "reaches". Canoes following a lee shore in such conditions may be comfortable but should be wary of exposed sections, say alongside level, open fields, where they could be blown offshore. Consider taking a course as close as possible to the line of the wind's direction on cross-lake legs. Canadian canoes when paddled solo are easily spun round by air currents. Typical periods of persistent RAIN cause lake levels to rise, allowing strong currents to run some way above the normal outflows. In MIST avoid busy jetties and do not venture across "shipping lanes" where steamers and motorboats ply. Keep a whistle to hand in poor visibility, in case mists form before you reach safety.

RIVERS flowing out of lakes can sweep a boat into various hazards - waterfalls, rocks, weirs, submerged ironwork - anything. Inspect outlets from a safe vantage point and be careful. Downstream-running is a committing but rewarding skill enjoyed mostly by kayakers. This area's definitive guidebook covering access, safety and technical aspects is *Rivers of Cumbria* (see appendix). But even careful owners of Canadian canoes might venture **upstream**. Heavy rains, raising lake levels above normal, followed by a short dry spell during which river flows abate, allow the canoeist to venture furthest up the "feeders". It's a challenge - if a relatively mild one - to see just how far you can paddle. And if you don't like the look of the next section you can turn and, without effort, practise some elementary river-running, knowing what's in store.

SWIMMING can appeal on a warm day. Comfortable water temperatures are rare in an English lake. When they do occur, colder pockets trap the unwary and kill strong men at all times of the year. Drownings usually take place during heat-waves. Stay within your depth. The level "beaches" always dip abruptly into very deep, very much cooler water. Here any poor swimmer will sink; anybody could have a heart attack. Responsible long-distance and cross-lake swimmers are accompanied by boats.

The "Better Drowned than Duffers" sentiments expressed in Arthur Ransome's stories are (sadly) out-moded. The message has to be: YOUNG CHILDREN should never go NEAR water - let alone on or in it - without constant supervision by a responsible and competent adult/swimmer.

ON THE WATER

NORTHERN LAKES

Distances indicate maximum inshore circuits and include round-island detours

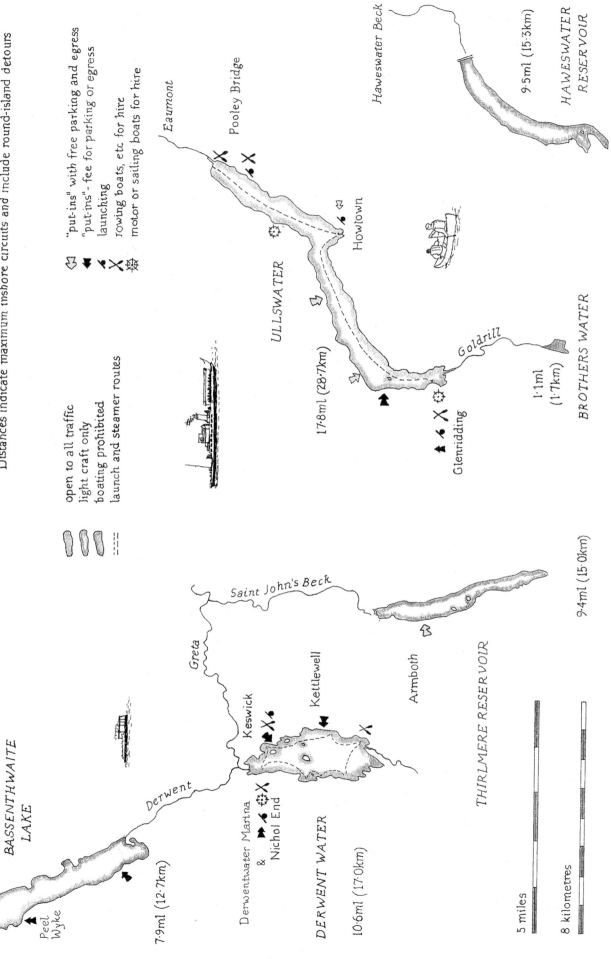

open to all traffic

light craft only

boating prohibited

launch and steamer routes

☜ "put-ins" with free parking and egress

▼ "put-ins" – fee for parking or egress

✕ launching

✕ rowing boats, etc for hire

⚙ motor or sailing boats for hire

BASSENTHWAITE LAKE

Ouse Bridge

Peel Wyke

7·9ml (12·7km)

Derwent

Greta

Keswick

Derwentwater Marina & Nichol End

DERWENT WATER

10·6ml (17·0km)

Kettlewell

Saint John's Beck

Armboth

THIRLMERE RESERVOIR

9·4ml (15·0km)

Eamont

Pooley Bridge

Howtown

ULLSWATER

17·8ml (28·7km)

Glenridding

Goldrill

1·1ml (1·7km)

BROTHERS WATER

Haweswater Beck

9·5ml (15·3km)

HAWESWATER RESERVOIR

5 miles

8 kilometres

14

MAPS and INFORMATION

NO ONE involved in the outdoors can pursue their activities safely or intelligently without an ORDNANCE SURVEY MAP. An up-to-date LANDRANGER at a scale of 1:50,000 (2cm to 1km) or the more convenient TOURIST ONE-INCH *LAKE DISTRICT* is best for planning and motoring, adding to the pleasure of a visit.

However the OUTDOOR LEISURE sheets at the larger scale of 1:25,000 (4cm to 1km or 2·5344 inches to the mile) are indispensable for use out-of-doors. FOUR of these double-sided maps cover the whole of the National Park plus a good way north and south to the Solway Plain and Morecambe Bay. Extremely detailed - showing every building and field; featuring rights-of-way, access areas, camping sites, information centres, car parks - they are incredible value. Distinguished by their bright yellow covers, they are readily available at information centres and post offices as well as bookshops and climbing equipment specialists. Each lake appears on an individual map as follows :

Windermere, Grasmere, Rydal Water, Elter Water, Esthwaite Water + north Coniston Water :-
Sheet No 7: *THE ENGLISH LAKES - SOUTH EASTERN AREA*

south Coniston Water and Wast Water :-
Sheet No 6: *SOUTH WESTERN AREA*

Ennerdale Water, Lowes Water, Crummock Water, Buttermere,
Bassenthwaite Lake and Derwent Water :-
Sheet No 4: *NORTH WESTERN AREA*

Thirlmere Reservoir, Brothers Water, Ullswater and Haweswater Reservoir :-
Sheet No 5: *NORTH EASTERN AREA*

The CHARTS in this book are designed to enhance their users' enjoyment of the Lakes by supplementing the definitive, accurate Ordnance Survey maps and not replacing them. For example, the O.S. National Grid system is the standard means of reference used by Rescue Services and others to identify the locations of casualties, incidents, rendezvous, etc. Every effort has been made to ensure information was correct and up-to-date prior to publication. Inevitably changes occur as any book or map goes to press. Treat information about transport, accommodation and services as a guide only. Apart from closure or change of use, public access, facilities and businesses may be subject to seasonal variation in opening times. The "Season" for lake transport, visitor centres and suchlike usually includes the Easter period and generally runs from early May until late October.

Keep up-to-date with a visit to the helpful staff at the well-stocked TOURIST INFORMATION OFFICES (see appendix). Ask them for one of the series of National Park Authority *Lake User's Guide* leaflets which indispensably up-date regulations, access and advice for visitors to Windermere, Coniston Water, Bassenthwaite Lake, Derwent Water and Ullswater.

Nine or ten associated clubs of the BRITISH CANOE UNION (see appendix) are based in Cumbria. In common with Outdoor Centres, they provide a safe introduction to all disciplines of canoeing and organise meets and competitions. Access to and use of waterways in Britain is somewhat complicated. On behalf of its members and others this national body negotiates and informs of regulations and restrictions pertaining to rivers, lakes and canals. The *BCU Yearbook* (free to members) provides details on access, club organisation and the myriad canoeing and kayaking activities.

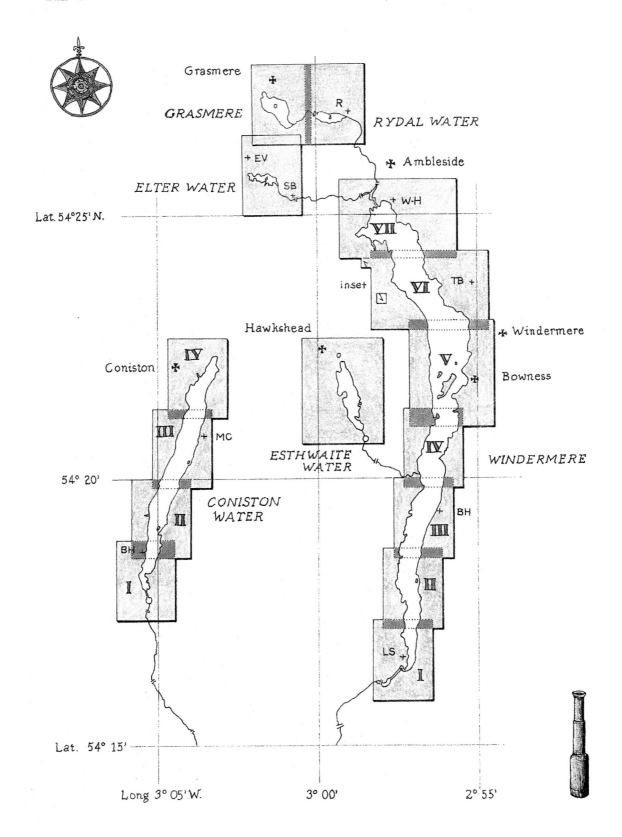

Grasmere

GRASMERE

R +

RYDAL WATER

+ EV

✠ Ambleside

ELTER WATER

SB

+ W-H

Lat. 54°25' N.

VII

inset

VI

TB +

Hawkshead

✠ Windermere

Coniston

IV

✠

✠ Bowness

V.

Esthwaite

ESTHWAITE WATER

III

+ MC

IV

WINDERMERE

54° 20'

II

CONISTON WATER

+ BH

III

BH +

II

I

LS +

I

Lat. 54° 15'

Long 3° 05' W.

3° 00'

2° 55'

THE CHARTS

THE CHARTS are based on the ORDNANCE SURVEY (national cartographic agency) 1:10,000 series plans. All the new and altered detail plus features not depicted on O.S. mapping were surveyed and compiled by the author during an exploration of the shores or adjacent roads and paths during 1997 - 2000.

ACCESS: In principle Coloured features on the Charts denote: (a) Areas where public access appeared to be established; (b) Public or permitted roads, paths and rights-of-way; (c) Buildings with public facilities or establishments catering for visitors. Note that un-coloured features denote private property or areas closed to the general public. (Exceptionally all water and rock features are coloured to give the Charts some continuity.)

Please observe any restrictions in force at the time of your visit. For example, some facilities may be subject to opening hours. The inclusion of a road or path on a Chart does not guarantee legal access. Rights-of-way depicted on Ordnance Survey maps are subject to change of status or extent. Act with due respect and consideration on all property, whether private or public.

Only recognised and designated lay-bys or car parks and convenient-for-all put-ins have been included. Although other locations might appear feasible for these purposes, please do not impede or cause inconvenience to workers or others by parking and launching indiscriminately.

FORMAT: The margins of the Charts are defined by lines of longitude (meridians) and latitude (parallels) at 10-second intervals. Values are given where space permits and lines drawn within lake areas at 30-second intervals. (See Scales and Orientation, below.)

The larger lakes require several Charts for complete coverage. Accordingly overlaps of 10, 20 or 30 seconds provide continuity for outdoor use. The extents of overlaps are indicated by breaks in the decorated margins. These breaks might simplify the assembly of component Charts onto a single sheet.

NAMES: *Italic lettering* has been adopted for *NATURAL FEATURES*. Names without capital letters are descriptive.

Preference is given to the standard practice which seeks to separate the elements of a place name where it refers to the original landmark. Subsequently that name might be compounded if it is adopted for an associated feature. For example, there is no doubt that "Red Beck" is a stream and "Redbeck", a settlement, is not. Furthermore, "Redbeck Bridge" looks tidier than "Red Beck Bridge". Such treatment would emphasise the significance of ancient words and obviate the confusions between lake and village suffered by - dare I suggest?- "Winder-mere / Winder Mere", "Gras-mere / Gras Mere", "Butter-mere/ Butter Mere" and their contiguous villages whose names are (properly) compounded.

HEIGHTING: Lake levels vary - on the larger ones, enormously. Since the 6th edition of the One-Inch Series the Ordnance Survey have no longer published the altitudes of water features on small-scale maps. Those adopted here are taken from 6th or older editions. In Scandinavia even road maps publish lake heights and indicate maximum - minimum levels where appropriate!

Please notice that on the Charts, figures relate to altitudes above and below individual lake levels - and not Mean Sea Level (the normal Ordnance Datum). Apart from hill tops, heightings have been selected to indicate the rise and fall along paths and roads for walkers and riders.

FLOATING OBJECTS, excepting jetties, are not depicted on these Charts. Such markers on the lakes' surfaces indicate moorings, distances, shallows, shipping lanes and yacht-racing courses. These and submarine contours and soundings appear on the excellent *Windermere Lake Chart* which is designed for sailing or motor-boating and published by the South Lakeland District Council.

A KEY to symbols and colours appears on page 21 and the rear endpaper.

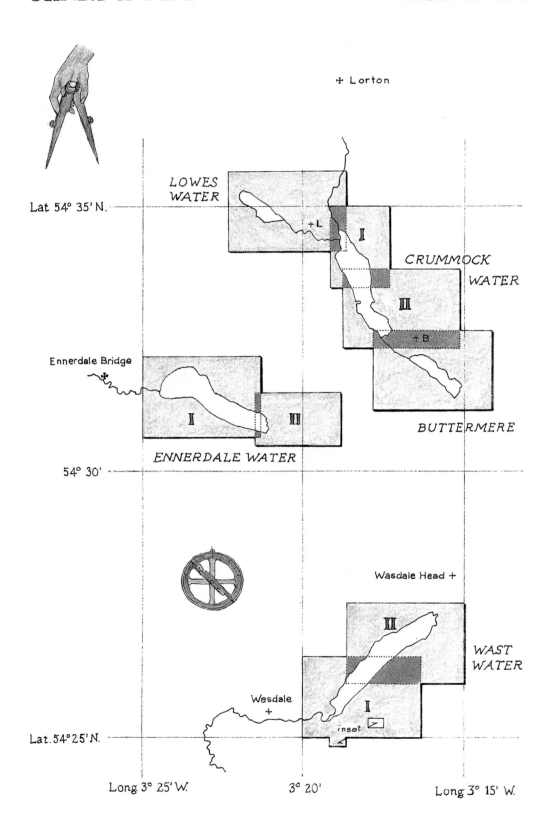

+ Lorton

Lat 54° 35' N.

LOWES
WATER

+ L

I

CRUMMOCK

WATER

III

+ B

Ennerdale Bridge

I

III

BUTTERMERE

ENNERDALE WATER

54° 30'

Wasdale Head +

III

WAST
WATER

Wasdale
+

I

inset

Lat. 54° 25' N.

Long 3° 25' W.   3° 20'   Long 3° 15' W.

SCALE and ORIENTATION

ONE Nautical Mile is the distance one minute of arc subtends on the Earth's surface from its centre along a Great Circle (e.g. lines of longitude and the Equator). The traditional distance passed down to the mariner was 6,080 feet (1,853·18 metres). This was abandoned for a figure of 6082 feet (1853·79m) until 1929 when the International Nautical Mile was fixed at 1852 metres (6076·12 ft) which accorded with the accepted circumference of the Earth.
Thus 40,003·2 km (24,856·9 mls) ÷ 360 degrees ÷ 60 minutes = 1852 metres.

The Charts are cast on the simplest Mercator projection. They are oriented to and defined by lines of longitude and latitude drawn at right angles with divisions along margins to indicate 10-second intervals.

Lines of latitude subtend a constant distance of 1012·66 feet (308·66 metres) between these divisions, i.e. one-sixth of a Nautical Mile. Longitude intervals shrink from this maximum distance at the Equator to zero at the Poles, where they converge. Consequently the distance across 10 seconds of latitude reduces from approximately 592 ft (180·4m) at Newby Bridge below Windermere to 586 ft (178·5m) at Ouse Bridge on Bassenthwaite Lake. However, any scale differences across the total width of a Chart is restricted to about 0·07 inches (1·5mm), the equivalent of 50 feet (15 metres) over land or water. As it is, much greater distortions are required to depict roads and congested areas clearly.

Lines of latitude and longitude appear at half-minute (30 second) intervals on the Charts in lake areas. These represent distances of 3038 ft = 0·575 miles (926m) and 1776-1758 ft = 0·337 miles (541-535m) respectively.

Scales representing nautical miles, statute miles and kilometres on the Charts appear below and on the rear endpaper.

In the Lake District the Compass is deflected by the Earth's magnetic field approximately 5° west of true north. This angle of deviation is decreasing by ½° every four years or so. Therefore true and magnetic north are due to coincide in the year 2040. In the meantime subtract the variation from actual bearings or sightings before applying them to a Chart. Conversely, add the variation to bearings taken from Charts when setting a course overland or across water. True or geographical north lies at the top of the Charts.

SCALES

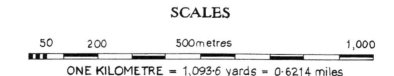

| 50 | 200 | 500metres | | 1,000 |

ONE KILOMETRE = 1,093·6 yards = 0·6214 miles

| 100 | 220 yards | 3 furlongs | 880 yards | 6 furlongs | 1,760 yds |

ONE MILE = 1,609·34 metres or 1·609 kilometres = 5,280 feet = 63,360 inches

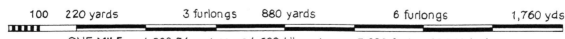

| 608 feet | 405 yds,1ft | ½ nautical ml | 800 fathoms | 100 cables |

OLD NAUTICAL MILE = 1,853·18 metres = 1 mile,266 yards,2 feet = 6,080 feet = 100 cables

CHART INDEX

NORTHERN LAKES

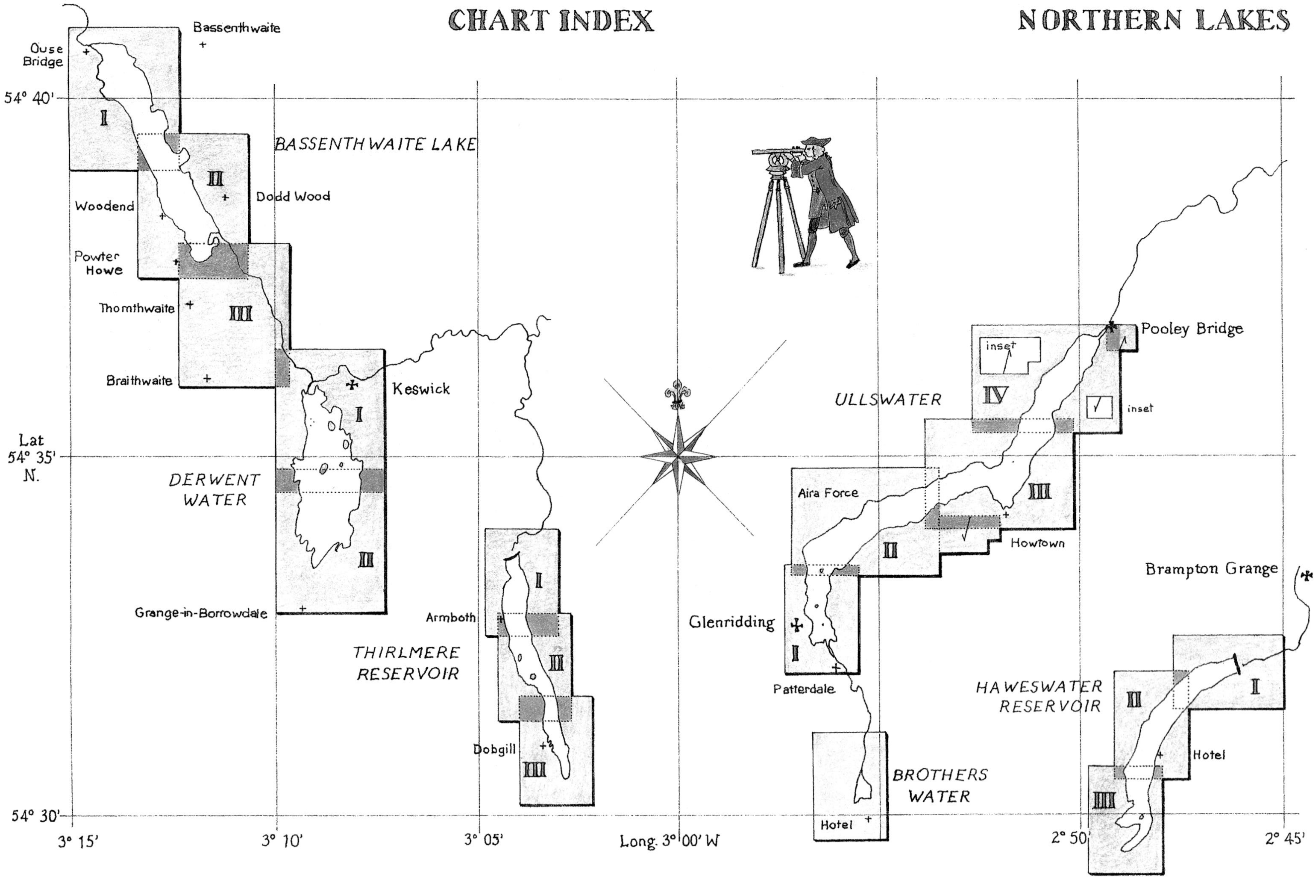

Ouse Bridge

BASSENTHWAITE LAKE

Bassenthwaite

Dodd Wood

Woodend

Powter Howe

Thornthwaite

Braithwaite

I

II

III

Keswick

I

III

DERWENT WATER

Grange-in-Borrowdale

Lat 54° 35' N.

54° 40'

54° 30'

3° 15'

3° 10'

3° 05'

THIRLMERE RESERVOIR

Armboth

Dobgill

II

III

III

Long. 3° 00' W

Pooley Bridge

inset

ULLSWATER

IV

inset V

III

Howtown

Aira Force

Glenridding

Patterdale

II

I

BROTHERS WATER

Hotel

Brampton Grange

I

Hotel

II

III

HAWESWATER RESERVOIR

2° 45'

2° 50'

20

LEGEND

N.B. Excepting rock and water, colour denotes public access or facilities. (See p 17.)

public ROAD: ~~~ TRACK: ~~~	PARKING: unrestricted	
PATH along private road, ~~~ track ~~~	PARKING: subject to charge	
surfaced ~~~ trodden ~~~ indistinct ~~~	BUS service 🚌 seasonal facility ◑	
steps ▦ gate ~~~ stile ~~~	picnic site ⊓ play area K	
wall ~~~ hedge ~~~ fence ++++	camping 🏕 tourers	
PASSENGER steamer, ◉ launch ◯	lawn, parkland National Trust land ❧	
canoe PUT-IN: free ▷ fee ▷	National Park ⊖ Forest Enterprise ♣	
LAUNCHING for sailing craft	building with PUBLIC FACILITIES	
stone embankment, quay	private house, outbuilding, boat house	
wooden landing stage ✗	toilets WC tourist info. office ℹ	
fixed danger marker ⚓ life-belt ◯	post office ✉ telephone kiosk × ✆	

woodland ♠♠ fir ♣♣♣ coppice	FOOD: eat "in" or "out"	
azalea etc.● gorse ❀ ❀ bracken etc.	restaurant ♟ café, teas ☕ pub, bar ℙ	
heath ~~~ cliff & rock ♫ ❦ scree	take-away ▼ shop ⚖ D.I.Y. ⊓	
WATER ☁ stream ~~~ marsh ~~~		
reeds ⸜ rocks ⸜ shingle	BOAT HIRE: motor ❂	
DON'T DISTURB...take care of the countryside !	sailing ⛵ rowing X	
wildfowl ✒ pasture ◠ crops	kayak / Canadian canoe \	

21

THE SOUTHERN LAKES
Some General Notes
plus
Supplementary Remarks to Lake Charts

THE TERRAIN enclosing this first ensemble of water is the most pastoral in the Lake District and serves as a gentle introduction to the more rugged, central mountains. The sedimentary rocks from which these hills were eroded are the softest and least ancient. Today's landscape is predominantly agricultural or heavily wooded. In ancient times great priories and abbeys benefited from the riches gained from farming and forestry. From prehistory until the Industrial Revolution the woodland maintained its importance, providing raw materials in support of iron production (ore and charcoal), basket-making (coppice), mining (charcoal for gunpowder and pit-props) and the cotton industry (bobbins), while mines and quarries exported copper, slate and stone down the convenient reaches of the larger lakes. Landings are discernible below the King's Wheel on the Brathay serving Windermere, while Kirby and Nibthwaite Quays acted as termini for goods ferried the length of Coniston Water.

The mountains defining the watershed of the Southern Lakes are composed of older, more durable volcanic rocks. Western and northern horizons of these waters are familiar to regular visitors. The characteristic shapes of Coniston Old Man, the Langdale Pikes, The Lion and the Lamb or the Fairfield Horseshoe provide dramatic backdrops for a shore wander or boat trip. Innumerable mountain becks or streams feed the lakes, and the picturesque Rothay and Brathay rivers link four of the half dozen in this group. The Leven and Crake, the outlets for Windermere and Coniston Water, flow into Morecambe Bay. The Duddon, with its much-praised though lakeless Valley, and the Kent on which stands Kendal, "Gateway to The Lakes", are the other chief rivers in this catchment area. (Abbot Hall, Kendal, has a section in the Museum of Lakeland Life devoted to Arthur Ransome, originator of *Swallows & Amazons*.)

Lying closest to the great urban centres, the Windermere area is served by the railway line plus fast, convenient, motorway-standard roads. As well as longer-term visitors, a consequence is the vast influx of day-trippers who expect more passive forms of tourist activities than hitherto provided or anticipated. Visiting the exhibitions and museums which abound is a more appropriate way of avoiding inclement weather than going shopping or being entertained. Some may believe modern presentation dumbs-down the information on hand but the messages remain, often with greater impact for the very young. During the ever-expanding "seasons" new visitors will not experience a better introduction to Windermere or Coniston Water than the special-interest excursions laid on by Windermere Lake Cruises and the Steamboat Museum or Gondola and Coniston Launch.

Between the two "great lakes" lies the Grisedale Forest. Until recently the Forestry Commission's policy protected its natural seclusion. Today facilities exist for visitors to leave their vehicles and cycle or ramble along way-marked routes between these shores and the Visitor Centre, which offers refreshment, camping, cycle-hire, exhibitions and sculpture-trails.

A few regular bus routes serve the shores. Several "Lakeslink" buses run every day along the highway from Kendal to Keswick via Windermere Station, Ambleside, Rydal and Grasmere village. In dry weather the Open-top model gives this journey along England's most beautiful highway extra dimension. Within the couple-a-day category, Windermere Station is linked to Newby Bridge, and Ambleside to Coniston village via Hawkshead by the "Coniston Rambler". A more regular service connects Coniston and Torver with Ulverston.

Accommodation in this area is welcoming, varied and plentiful. The choice ranges from tents to luxurious-but-charming hotels. Apart from a dearth of campsites in the vale of Grasmere/Rydal your lakeside sojourn may be taken in caravans, bunk-houses or hostels run by outdoor organisations, self-catering, B&Bs and inns. Such is the popularity of this region, it would be wise to secure your accommodation before arrival at weekends and during holidays.

The National Park Authority issues *Lake User's Guides* for Windermere and Coniston Water.

"It's a' nabs and neuks is Windermer'". Largest and most accessible of the lakes, WINDERMERE is inevitably the most popular and busiest. However Wordsworth's summary, "None of the other lakes unfold so many fresh beauties to him who sails upon them", still holds good two centuries on. Many neuks and rocky nabs remain in private grounds so, in the off-season at least, it is easy to imagine oneself paddling along some wilderness backwater.

The name means Vinander or Winander's Lake. Winander was a Norseman and "mere" is Old English (Anglo-Saxon) for lake. Therefore if off-comers, tourists, telly presenters and such-like talk about "Windermere lake", please realise they are saying Winder's Lake-lake! Should people need to avoid confusing this natural feature (named a thousand years ago) with the agglomeration of hotels, B&Bs, shops and houses that has spread (in the last 150 years) around the railway terminus at Birthwaite (christened Windermere Station), then let some appendage be applied to the name adopted for the built-up area. There'd be far less harm in "Windermere Town" or "Village" than the clumsy references made to the Mere of Winander. I may be labouring the point but the matter requires elucidation. Not that it is a very modern trend. Every lake has been subjected to such treatment ever since the earliest tourists responded to the Lake Poets' eulogies. Britain has scores of "River River"s, "Hill Hill"s and even a "Hill-Hill Hill". (Pendle Hill above Clitheroe in Lancashire is a repetition of Ancient British, Anglo-Saxon and Modern English.)

The southernmost limit and consequent length of Windermere is debateable. A very gradual flow commences below Fell Foot Park when the lake level is normal, but boats may ply up or down stream with scarcely any variation of effort. Indeed canoes take advantage of eddies to progress counter to the general current. The old County and Parish boundary is mered to "side of lake" and extends to the parapet of Newby Bridge. Here canoeists must assess their ability to paddle against the currents channelled between the buttresses before visiting more placid water above the weir. Below the weir the Leven's rapids meet the tidal reach in 2½ miles (4km). Some authorities state its name derives from the Welsh for "smooth", others from an Old English personal name. The Shallows, an ancient ford by the south end of Fell Foot Park, was dredged to allow boats access to the quays by the Swan Hotel. All-in-all, this section, which does run at an alarming rate after heavy rain, is regarded by boaters and treated on Chart I as an extension of Windermere. Not all the water in Windermere flows down the Leven. Some is extracted from the depths of the North Basin and pumped to the central treatment plant north of Kendal.

There are several easy-to-reach views of the lake. Motorists pull in to lay-bys on Beech Hill, Claife shore, Hammar Bank and Red Nab car parks. Handy spots to visit on foot other than those on the Charts are Biskey Howe in Bowness and Orrest Head above Windermere Station.

Yachting regattas began in 1818. The Royal Windermere Yacht Club (founded 1860) established their H.Q. in 1888. Boat-building had grown into an important local industry until the aftermath of the last war, when less traditional methods of production and changes in fashion put paid to the old boat-yards. The lake is deemed a highway for all craft subject to certain restrictions. BUY the local authority's excellent and indispensable lake chart "Windermere" for a modest sum - it is the most convenient for yachtsmen and owners of motorised craft. It updates the facilities necessary for launching and servicing such vessels and outlines the regulations for all lake-users. In summer two recently-introduced passenger ferries operate. One links Fell Foot Park and Lakeside Steamer Quay at the foot of the lake; the other, Bowness Piers and the Claife terminus of the vehicle ferry. This vessel, the *Brittania*, has a short rest and annual service during late autumn.

Before local government was re-organised in 1974 the bed of Windermere was part of the Parish of Bowness-on-Windermere, i.e. within the County of Westmorland. Current "ownership" of the bed and the surface of the lake rests with the District and County Councils respectively. The old part of Bowness is known as Lowfield. Belle Isle, re-named after Isabella Curwen, its owner, is the largest in the Lakes. During the Civil War the island resisted Roundhead attack for 8 months. The Round House was referred to as the "tea caddy" when it was constructed in 1774. Storrs Hall was built in the style of an Italian mansion. It was the meeting place of Sir Walter Scott and the Lake Poets in 1825. During the Industrial Revolution prospering captains of industry erected other great houses on Windermere's shores. Some commuted aboard their private steamships to Lakeside Station. The story of the establishment and changes of use of Belsfield, Fell Foot, Wray Castle and other edifices is fascinating.

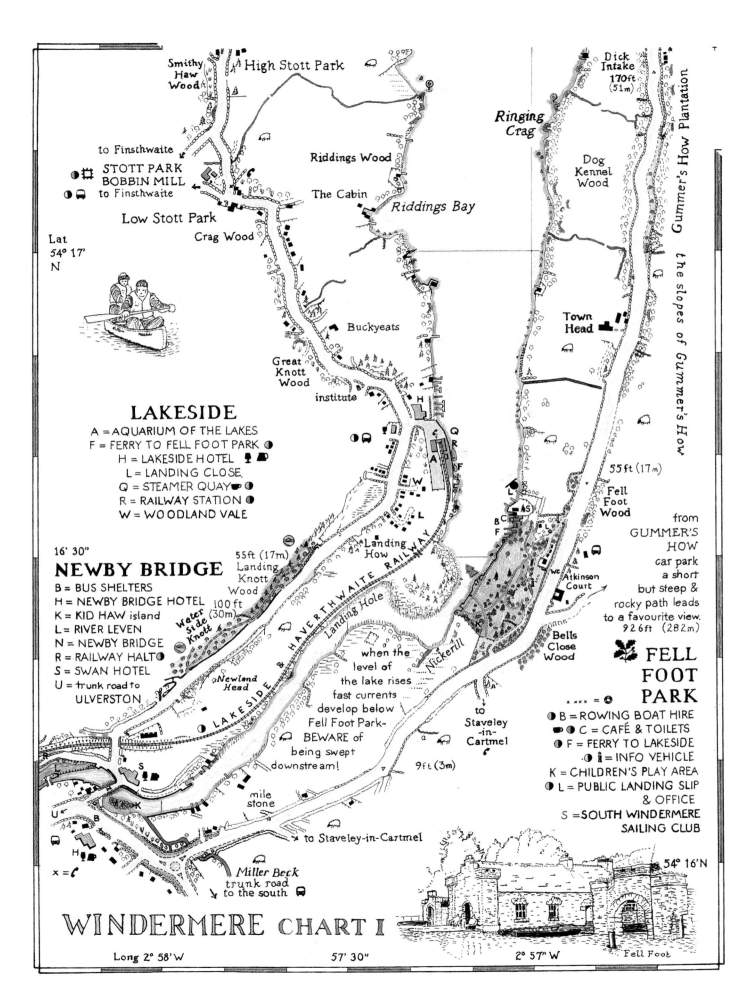

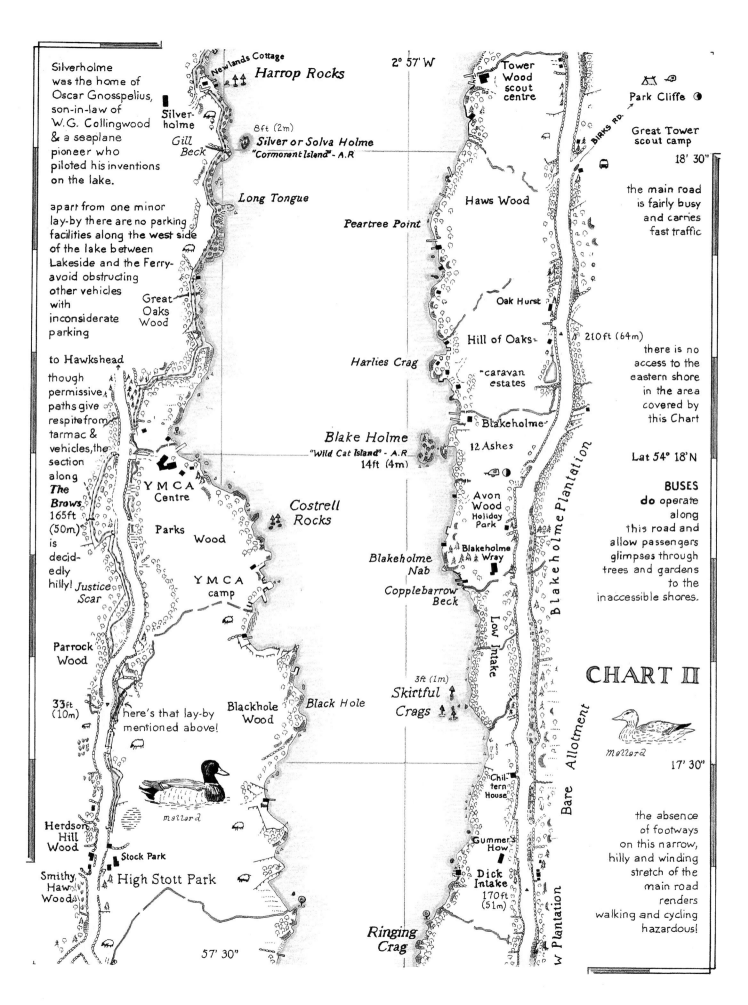

Silverholme was the home of Oscar Gnosspelius, son-in-law of W.G. Collingwood & a seaplane pioneer who piloted his inventions on the lake.

apart from one minor lay-by there are no parking facilities along the west side of the lake between Lakeside and the Ferry- avoid obstructing other vehicles with inconsiderate parking

to Hawkshead

though permissive paths give respite from tarmac & vehicles, the section along *The Brows* 165ft (50m) is decid- edly hilly!

Justice Scar

Parrock Wood

33ft (10m)

here's that lay-by mentioned above!

mallard

Herdson Hill Wood

Smithy Haw Wood

Stock Park

High Stott Park

Newlands Cottage

Harrop Rocks

Silver- holme

Gill Beck

8ft (2m)

Silver or Solva Holme "Cormorant Island" - A.R

Long Tongue

Great Oaks Wood

Peartree Point

Costrell Rocks

Parks Wood

Y M C A Centre

Y M C A camp

Blackhole Wood

Black Hole

2° 57′ W

Tower Wood scout centre

Haws Wood

BIRKS RD.

Oak Hurst

Hill of Oaks

210ft (64m)

Harlies Crag

caravan estates

Blakeholme

Blake Holme "Wild Cat Island" - A.R 14ft (4m)

12 Ashes

Avon Wood Holiday Park

Blakeholme Nab

Blakeholme Wray

Copplebarrow Beck

Low Intake

3ft (1m)

Skirtful Crags

Chil- tern House

Gummer's How

Dick Intake 170ft (51m)

Ringing Crag

Blakeholme Plantation

Bare Allotment

w Plantation

Park Cliffe

Great Tower scout camp

18′ 30″

the main road is fairly busy and carries fast traffic

there is no access to the eastern shore in the area covered by this Chart

Lat 54° 18′N

BUSES do operate along this road and allow passengers glimpses through trees and gardens to the inaccessible shores.

CHART II

mallard

17′ 30″

the absence of footways on this narrow, hilly and winding stretch of the main road renders walking and cycling hazardous!

57′ 30″

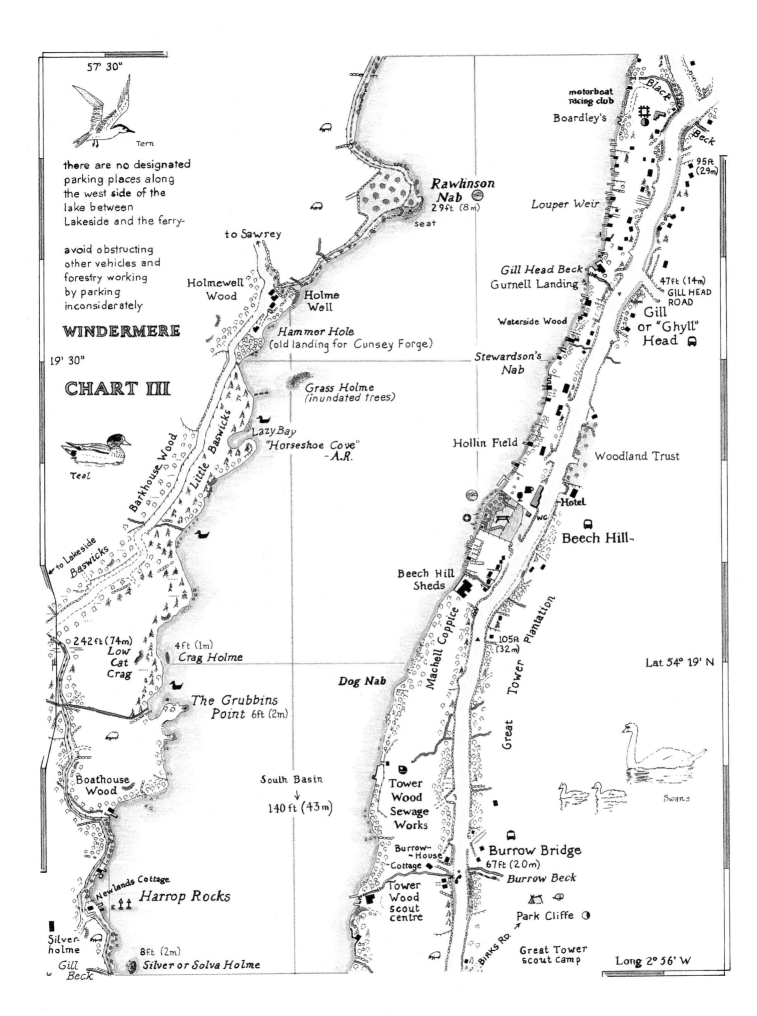

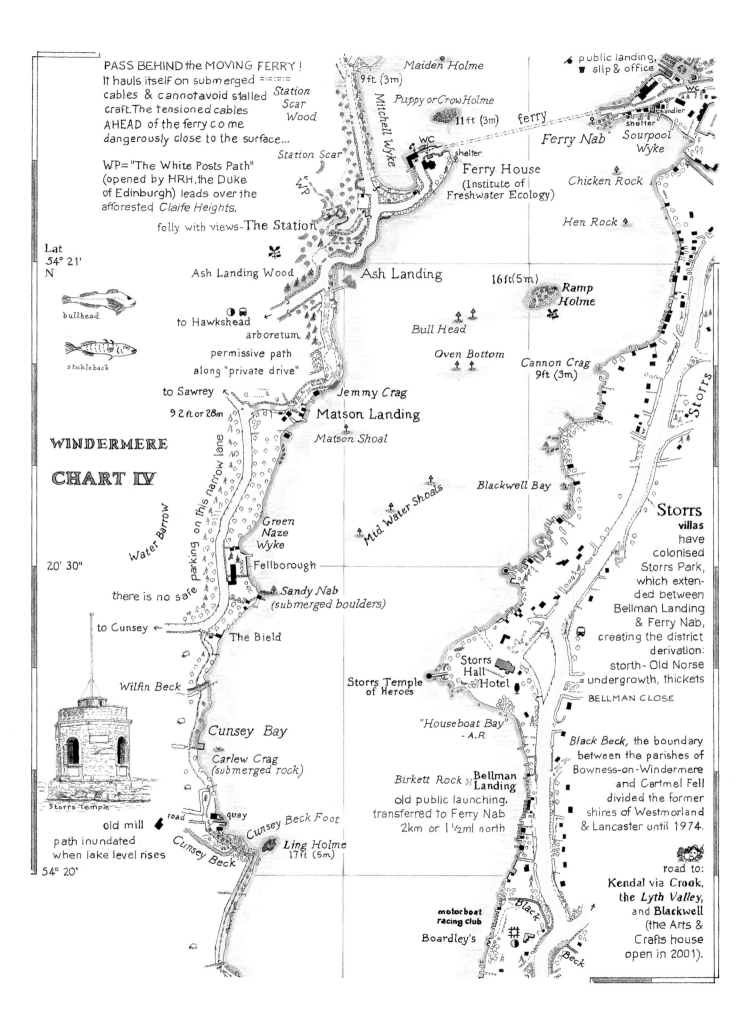

PASS BEHIND the MOVING FERRY!
It hauls itself on submerged
cables & cannot avoid stalled
craft. The tensioned cables
AHEAD of the ferry come
dangerously close to the surface...

WP = "The White Posts Path"
(opened by HRH, the Duke
of Edinburgh) leads over the
afforested *Claife Heights*.

folly with views - The Station

Station Scar Wood

Station Scar

WP

Lat 54° 21' N

bullhead

stickleback

WINDERMERE
CHART IV

20' 30"

Water Barrow

there is no safe parking on this narrow lane

to Cunsey ←

to Hawkshead

arboretum

permissive path
along "private drive"

to Sawrey
9.2 ft or 28m

Ash Landing Wood

Ash Landing

Jemmy Crag

Matson Landing

Matson Shoal

Green Naze Wyke

Fellborough

Sandy Nab
(submerged boulders)

The Bield

Wilfin Beck

Cunsey Bay

Carlew Crag
(submerged rock)

old mill
path inundated
when lake level rises

Storrs Temple

road

quay

Cunsey Beck Foot

Cunsey Beck

Ling Holme
17ft (5m)

54° 20'

Maiden Holme
9 ft (3m)

Mitchell Wyke

Puppy or Crow Holme

11 ft (3m)   ferry

WC   shelter

Ferry House
(Institute of
Freshwater Ecology)

Ferry Nab

Sourpool Wyke

public landing,
slip & office

WC

shelter

chandler

Chicken Rock

Hen Rock

16 ft (5m)

Ramp Holme

Bull Head

Oven Bottom

Cannon Crag
9ft (3m)

Blackwell Bay

Mid Water Shoals

Storrs

Storrs Hall Hotel

Storrs Temple
of Heroes

"Houseboat Bay"
- A.R

Birkett Rock

Bellman Landing
old public launching,
transferred to Ferry Nab
2km or 1½ml north

motorboat
racing club
Boardley's

Black Beck

Storrs
villas
have
colonised
Storrs Park,
which exten-
ded between
Bellman Landing
& Ferry Nab,
creating the district
derivation:
storth- Old Norse
undergrowth, thickets

BELLMAN CLOSE

Black Beck, the boundary
between the parishes of
Bowness-on-Windermere
and Cartmel Fell
divided the former
shires of Westmorland
& Lancaster until 1974.

road to:
Kendal via **Crook,**
the *Lyth Valley,*
and **Blackwell**
(the Arts &
Crafts house
open in 2001).

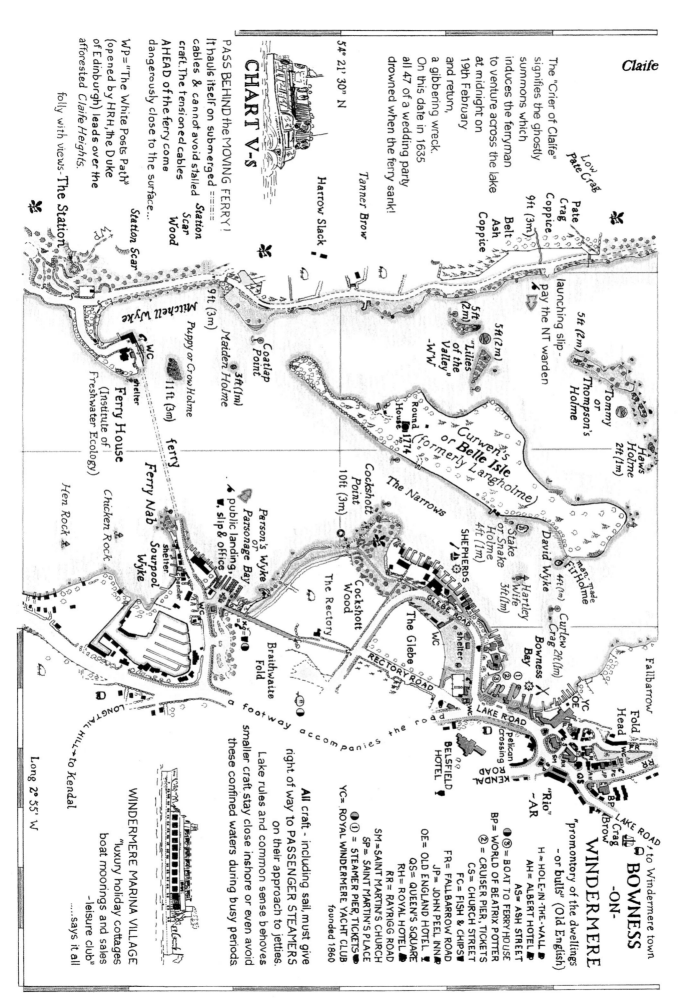

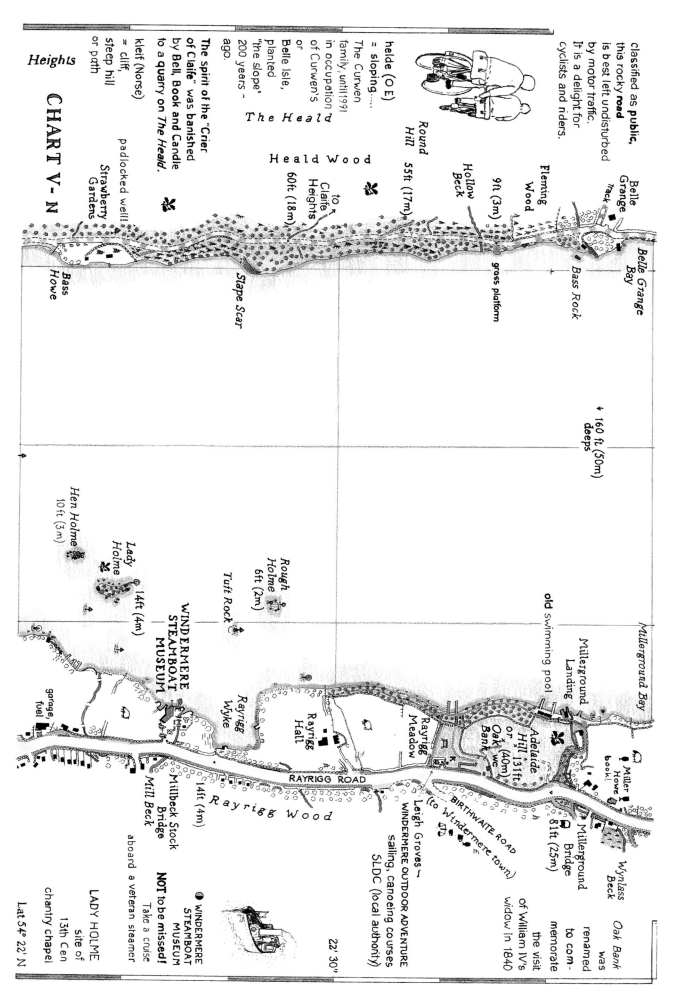

classified as **public**, this rocky **road** is best left undisturbed by motor traffic. It is a delight for cyclists and riders.

The Heald

helde (O E) = sloping..... The Curwen family, until 1991 in occupation of Curwen's or Belle Isle, planted "the slope" 200 years ago.

The spirit of the "Crier of Claife" was banished by Bell, Book and Candle to a quarry on *The Heald*.

Heights

kleif (Norse) = cliff, steep hill or path

CHART V - N

Belle Grange Bay
Belle Grange track
Bass Rock
grass platform
Fleming Wood
Hollow Beck
9ft (3m)
Round Hill 55ft (17m)
Heald Wood
60ft (18m)
to Claife Heights
Stape Scar
Bass Howe
Strawberry Gardens
padlocked well!

160 ft (50m) deeps

old swimming pool

Millerground Bay
Millerground Landing
Oak Bank was renamed to commemorate the visit of William IV's widow in 1840
Miller Howe book!
Wynlass Beck
Millerground Bridge 81ft (25m)
Adelaide Hill 131ft (40m) Oak wc Bank
Rayrigg Meadow
Leigh Groves ~ WINDERMERE OUTDOOR ADVENTURE sailing, canoeing courses SLDC (local authority)
BIRTHWAITE ROAD (to Windermere town)
RAYRIGG ROAD
Rayrigg Hall
Rayrigg Wyke
Rayrigg Wood
WINDERMERE STEAMBOAT MUSEUM
Tuft Rock
Rough Holme 6ft (2m)
Lady Holme 14ft (4m)
Hen Holme 10ft (3m)
14ft (4m)
garage, fuel
Mill Beck
Millbeck Stock Bridge
aboard a veteran steamer Take a cruise

● WINDERMERE STEAMBOAT MUSEUM **NOT** to be missed!

22' 30"

LADY HOLME site of 13th Cen chantry chapel

Lat 54° 22' N

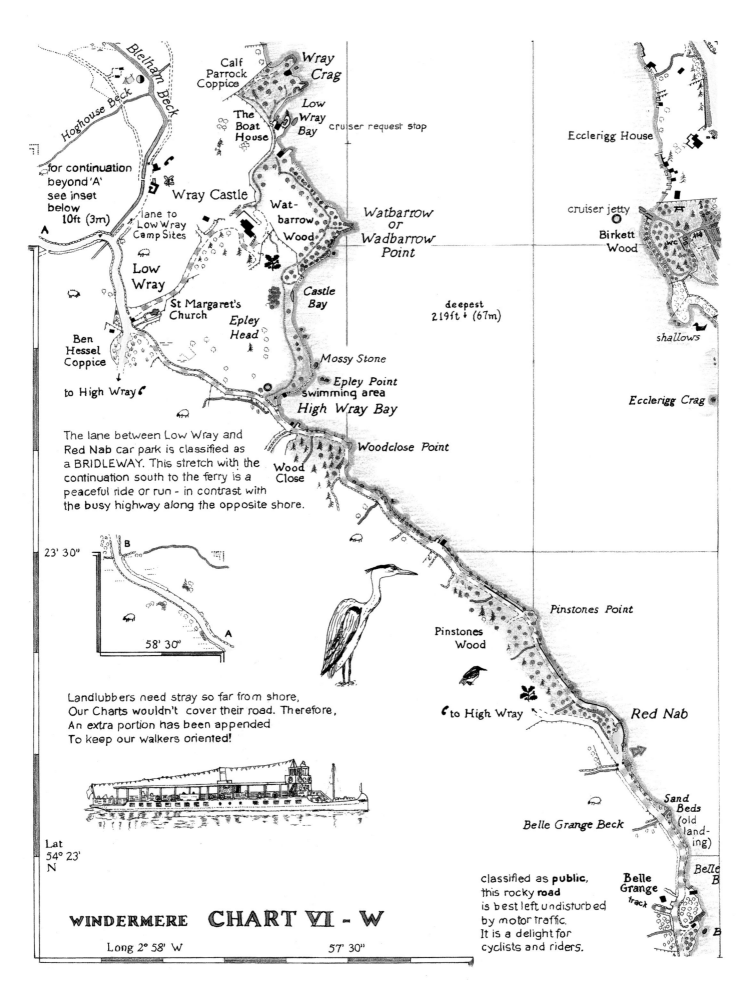

Blelham Beck

Hoghouse Beck

Calf Parrock Coppice

Wray Crag

Low Wray Bay

cruiser request stop

The Boat House

for continuation beyond 'A' see inset below 10ft (3m)

A

Wray Castle

lane to Low Wray Camp Sites

Wat-barrow Wood

Watbarrow or Wadbarrow Point

Low Wray

St Margaret's Church

Castle Bay

Epley Head

deepest 219ft ↨ (67m)

Ben Hessel Coppice

to High Wray

Mossy Stone

Epley Point

swimming area

High Wray Bay

The lane between Low Wray and Red Nab car park is classified as a BRIDLEWAY. This stretch with the continuation south to the ferry is a peaceful ride or run - in contrast with the busy highway along the opposite shore.

Woodclose Point

Wood Close

23' 30"

B

58' 30"

A

Ecclerigg House

cruiser jetty

Birkett Wood

wc

shallows

Ecclerigg Crag

Pinstones Point

Pinstones Wood

to High Wray

Landlubbers need stray so far from shore,
Our Charts wouldn't cover their road. Therefore,
An extra portion has been appended
To keep our walkers oriented!

Red Nab

Sand Beds (old landing)

Belle Grange Beck

Belle B

Lat 54° 23' N

classified as **public**, this rocky **road** is best left undisturbed by motor traffic. It is a delight for cyclists and riders.

Belle Grange track

B

Long 2° 58' W   57' 30"

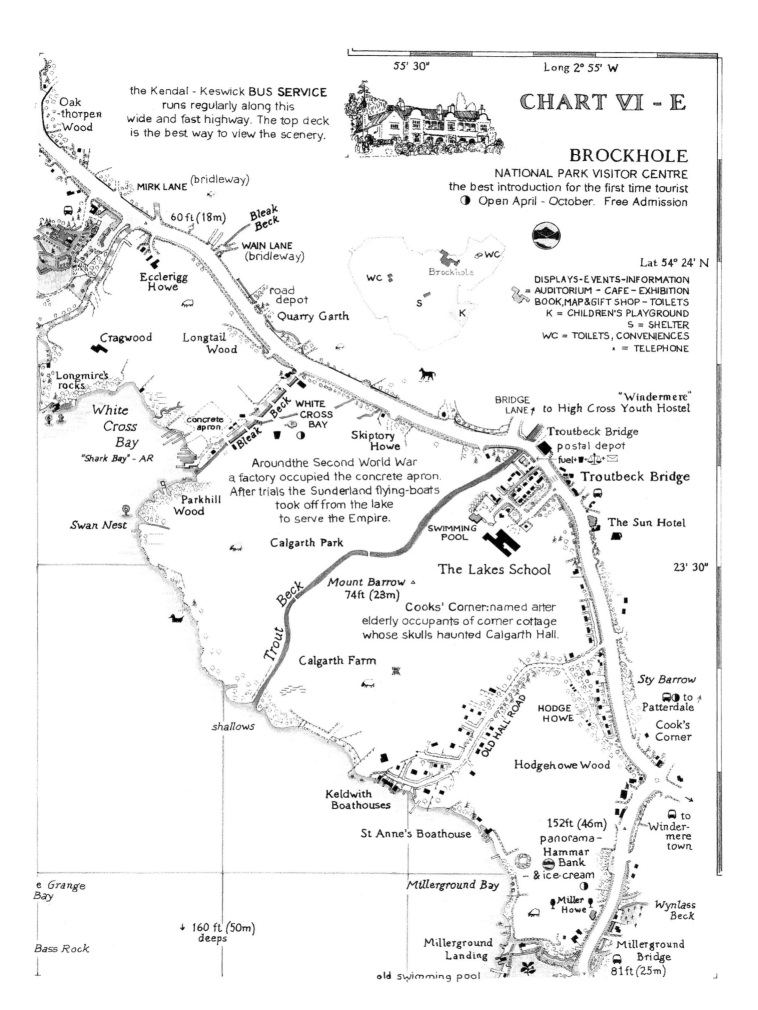

CHART VI – E

BROCKHOLE

NATIONAL PARK VISITOR CENTRE
the best introduction for the first time tourist
◗ Open April – October. Free Admission

Lat 54° 24' N

DISPLAYS – EVENTS – INFORMATION
= AUDITORIUM – CAFE – EXHIBITION
BOOK, MAP & GIFT SHOP – TOILETS
K = CHILDREN'S PLAYGROUND
S = SHELTER
WC = TOILETS, CONVENIENCES
⊠ = TELEPHONE

the Kendal - Keswick BUS **SERVICE**
runs regularly along this
wide and fast highway. The top deck
is the best way to view the scenery.

Oak
-thorpen
Wood

MIRK LANE (bridleway)

60 ft (18m)

Bleak Beck

WAIN LANE
(bridleway)

road
depot
Quarry Garth

Ecclerigg
Howe

Cragwood   Longtail
Wood

Longmire's
rocks

*White
Cross
Bay*

"Shark Bay" - AR

concrete
apron

Bleak Beck

WHITE
CROSS
BAY

Skiptory
Howe

Aroundthe Second World War
a factory occupied the concrete apron.
After trials the Sunderland flying-boats
took off from the lake
to serve the Empire.

Parkhill
Wood

Swan Nest

Calgarth Park

Trout Beck

Mount Barrow ₐ
74ft (23m)

Cooks' Corner: named after
elderly occupants of corner cottage
whose skulls haunted Calgarth Hall.

Calgarth Farm

shallows

BRIDGE
LANE ⌐

"Windermere"
to High Cross Youth Hostel

Troutbeck Bridge
postal depot
fuel ⊞ + ⚖ + ⊠

Troutbeck Bridge

The Sun Hotel

23' 30"

SWIMMING
POOL

The Lakes School

OLD HALL ROAD

HODGE
HOWE

Sty Barrow

🚌◗ to
Patterdale

Cook's
Corner

Hodgehowe Wood

🚌 to
Winder-
mere
town

Keldwith
Boathouses

St Anne's Boathouse

152ft (46m)
panorama –
Hammar
Bank
– & ice-cream

Millerground Bay

Miller
Howe

Wynlass
Beck

e Grange
Bay

Bass Rock

↓ 160 ft (50m)
deeps

Millerground
Landing

Millerground
Bridge
81 ft (25m)

old swimming pool

WC   ⍟ WC
Brockhole
WC ⍟
S ⍟
K

31

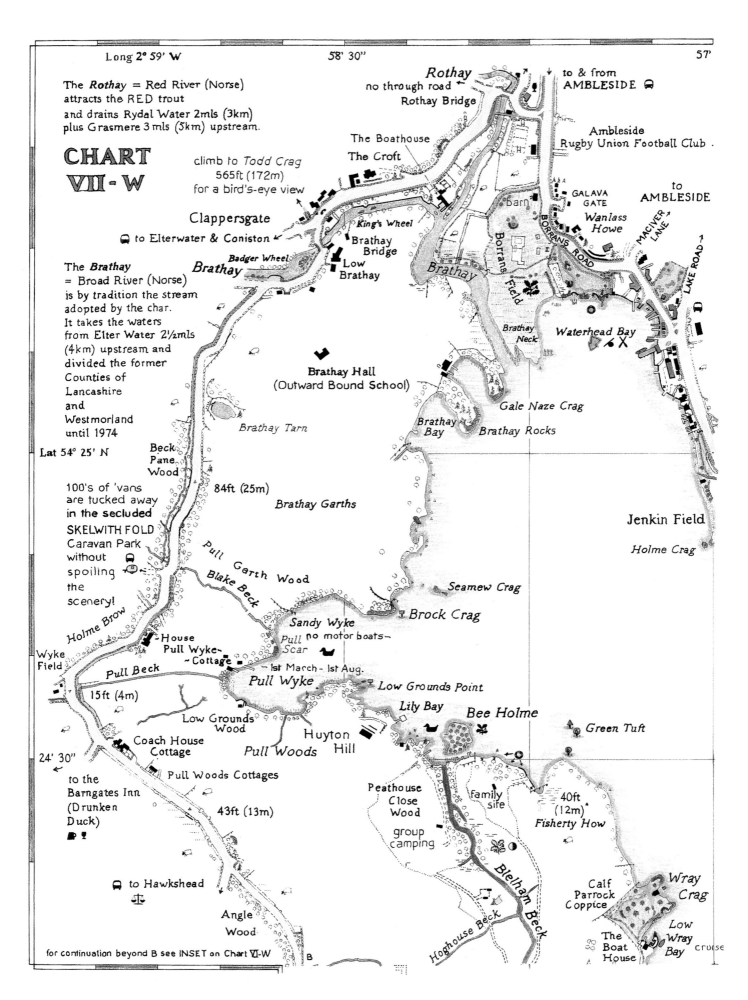

The *Rothay* = Red River (Norse)
attracts the RED trout
and drains Rydal Water 2mls (3km)
plus Grasmere 3 mls (5km) upstream.

CHART
VII - W

Rothay
no through road ←
Rothay Bridge

to & from
AMBLESIDE

climb to *Todd Crag*
565ft (172m)
for a bird's-eye view

The Boathouse
The Croft

Ambleside
Rugby Union Football Club .

Clappersgate

🚌 to Elterwater & Coniston ←

King's Wheel

Brathay
Bridge

Badger Wheel

Low
Brathay

Brathay

to
AMBLESIDE

GALAVA
GATE
Wanlass
Howe

Barn

Borrans Field

BORRANS ROAD

MACIVER LANE

LAKE ROAD

The *Brathay*
= Broad River (Norse)
is by tradition the stream
adopted by the char.
It takes the waters
from Elter Water 2½mls
(4km) upstream and
divided the former
Counties of
Lancashire
and
Westmorland
until 1974

Brathay

Brathay
Neck

Waterhead Bay

Brathay Hall
(Outward Bound School)

Brathay
Bay

Gale Naze Crag

Brathay Rocks

Lat 54° 25' N

Brathay Tarn

Beck
Pane
Wood

100's of 'vans
are tucked away
in the secluded
SKELWITH FOLD
Caravan Park
without
spoiling
the
scenery!

84ft (25m)

Brathay Garths

Jenkin Field

Holme Crag

Pull Garth Wood

Blake Beck

Seamew Crag

Holme Brow

Brock Crag

Sandy Wyke

*Pull
Scar*

no motor boats

Wyke
Field

—House
Pull Wyke~
~Cottage

1st March - 1st Aug.

Pull Wyke

Pull Beck

Low Grounds Point

15ft (4m)

Low Grounds
Wood

Lily Bay

Bee Holme

Green Tuft

Coach House
Cottage

Pull Woods

Huyton
Hill

24' 30"

←

to the
Barngates Inn
(Drunken
Duck)

Pull Woods Cottages

43ft (13m)

Peathouse
Close
Wood

family
site

40ft
(12m)
Fisherty How

group
camping

🚌 to Hawkshead

Angle
Wood

Bleiham Beck

Calf
Parrock
Coppice

Wray
Crag

The
Boat
House

*Low
Wray
Bay*

Hoghouse Beck

cruise

for continuation beyond B see INSET on Chart VI-W

B

WINDERMERE
CHART VII-E

Statistics
length: 11mls 420yds (18·08km)
width: 1630yds (1·49km)
max depth: 219ft (67m)
av depth: 78ft (24m)
surface level: 128ft (39m)
area: 5·69sq mls (14·73sq km)

GALAVA ROMAN FORT
in "Borrans Field"

〰〰〰	1ST CEN DITCH
- - - - -	2ND CEN WALL
I	HEAD QUARTERS
II	COMMANDER'S HOUSE
III	GRANARY
IV	DOUBLE PORTAL
V	TOWERS
VI	SOUTH GATE
——	MODERN FEATURES

Borrans = pile of stones (Norse)

AMBLESIDE, a mile north of Waterhead, offers a choice of comfortable hotels, guest houses, restaurants and a fish-and-chip shop. A reasonable range of shops caters for residents, although walkers, climbers and cyclists buying or hiring gear are well served by established outlets.

Charlotte Mason College on Rydal Road houses a climbing wall, but more appropriately for this publication, the ARMITT MUSEUM. Displays feature: the life and work of John Ruskin - art historian and philosopher; the Collingwood family - artists, historians, archeologists, etc; Oscar Gnosspelius- seaplane pioneer- who married a Collingwood; Beatrix Potter's natural history watercolours; early local photographs; a model of the Roman fort of GALAVA - with "finds" from R.G. Collingwood's excavations of 1913-1920.

KEY to WATERHEAD's facilities

path to Jenkyn's Crag (view)

Stencher Beck

Dove Nest Wood

Thief Fold Wood
kiln

Wansfell
Boathouse

Dove Nest Bay

Fisher Beck

Birdhouse Meadow
(conservation area)

Borrans Park

hotels

WC & 🚻

s = shelter

Waterhead Hotel

public slip (fee)
public jetty (2 hr limit)
rowing boat hire
lake cruisers
steamer pier & booking

Ambleside Youth Hostel

Fuel

9ft (3m)

path to Skell Gill
The Low Wood Hotel

mile stone

Holbeck Bridge
Hol Beck

Holbeck Point

HOLBECK LANE
to Troutbeck

Langdale Chase Hotel

Oak-thorpen Wood

Ecclerigg House

the Kendal - Keswick **BUS SERVICE** runs regularly along this wide and fast highway. The top deck is the best way to view the scenery.

24' 30"

cruiser request stop

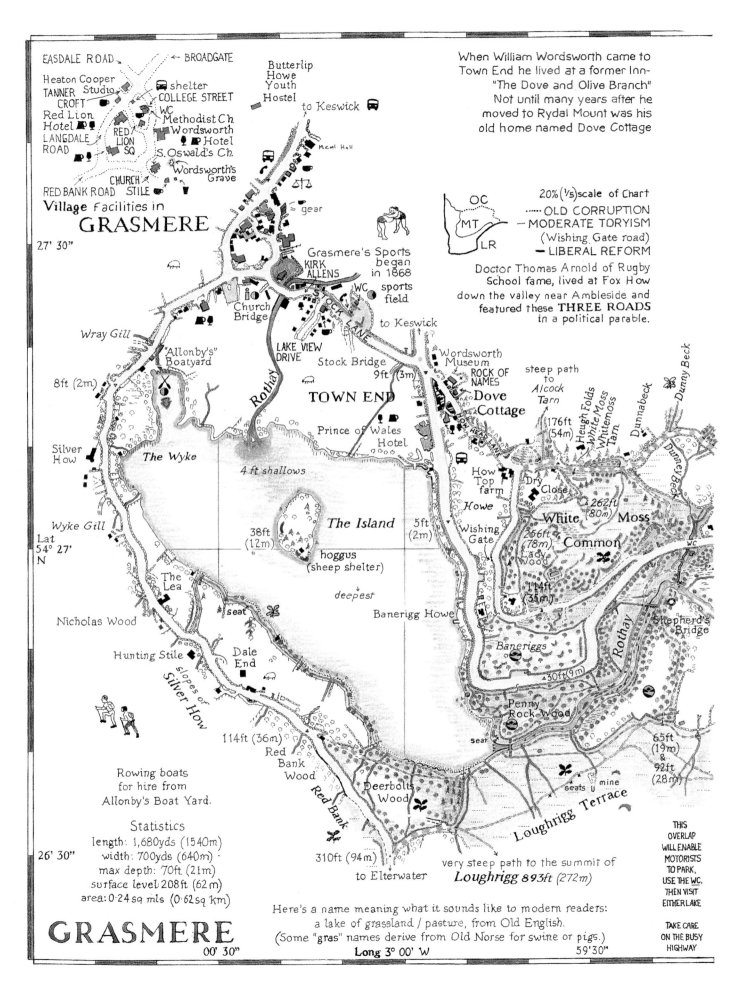

Village Facilities in
GRASMERE

EASDALE ROAD ← BROADGATE
Heaton Cooper Studio
TANNER CROFT
Red Lion Hotel
LANGDALE ROAD
RED LION SQ
shelter
COLLEGE STREET
WC
Methodist Ch
Wordsworth Hotel
S. Oswald's Ch.
Wordsworth's Grave
CHURCH STILE
RED BANK ROAD

Butterlip Howe Youth Hostel
to Keswick
Mem! Hall
gear

27' 30"

When William Wordsworth came to Town End he lived at a former Inn – "The Dove and Olive Branch" Not until many years after he moved to Rydal Mount was his old home named Dove Cottage

OC
MT
LR
20% (⅕) scale of Chart
······ OLD CORRUPTION
— MODERATE TORYISM
  (Wishing Gate road)
— LIBERAL REFORM

Doctor Thomas Arnold of Rugby School fame, lived at Fox How down the valley near Ambleside and featured these **THREE ROADS** in a political parable.

Grasmere's Sports began in 1868
KIRK ALLENS
WC
sports field
to Keswick

Wray Gill
"Allonby's" Boatyard
Church Bridge
LAKE VIEW DRIVE
Rothay
Stock Bridge
9ft (3m)
TOWN END
Prince of Wales Hotel
Wordsworth Museum
ROCK OF NAMES
Dove Cottage
steep path to Alcock Tarn
176ft (54m)
Heugh Folds
White Moss
Whitemoss Tarn
Dunnabeck
Dunny Beck

8ft (2m)

Silver How
The Wyke
4 ft shallows
How Top farm
Howe
Wishing Gate
Lady Wood
Dry Close
262ft (80m)
266ft (78m)
White Moss Common
114ft (35m)
WC

Wyke Gill
Lat 54° 27' N
The Island
38ft (12m)
hoggus (sheep shelter)
5ft (2m)
deepest
Banerigg Howe
Baneriggs
30ft (9m)
Rothay
Shepherd's Bridge

The Lea
Nicholas Wood
Hunting Stile
Dale End
seat
Penny Rock Wood
65ft (19m) & 92ft (28m)

slopes of Silver How
114ft (36m)
Red Bank Wood
Deerbolts Wood
seats
mine
Loughrigg Terrace

Rowing boats for hire from Allonby's Boat Yard.

Statistics
length: 1,680yds (1540m)
width: 700yds (640m)
max depth: 70ft (21m)
surface level: 208ft (62m)
area: 0·24 sq mls (0·62 sq km)

26' 30"

Red Bank
310ft (94m)
to Elterwater
very steep path to the summit of *Loughrigg* 893ft (272m)

Here's a name meaning what it sounds like to modern readers: a lake of grassland / pasture, from Old English. (Some "gras" names derive from Old Norse for swine or pigs.)

THIS OVERLAP WILL ENABLE MOTORISTS TO PARK, USE THE WC. THEN VISIT EITHER LAKE

TAKE CARE ON THE BUSY HIGHWAY

GRASMERE
00' 30"
Long 3° 00' W
59'30"

27' 30"

Grasmere

The Grasmere and Rydal area is exceptionally beautiful and justifiably world-renowned. Both its intimate scenery and literary associations attract all types of visitor. Easy walking circuits can be devised using a combination of varied footways. The busy highway between Ambleside and Keswick gives motorists the surprise view of *Grasmere* backed by the *"Lion and the Lamb"* mountain on their northward journey. People from all over the world visit the homes and resting places of William Wordsworth and his coterie of Lake Poets. The waters of Grasmere and the southern half of Rydal Water are leased by Lowther Estates to the National Trust. Northern Rydal Water forms part of the Rydal Hall estate. The le Fleming family, who had developed a 16th Cen farmhouse into an elegant, stately mansion, leased then finally sold the property to the Diocese of Carlisle in 1970. A variety of accommodation is available for individuals or groups seeking retreat, study and recreation (including canoeing the Water).

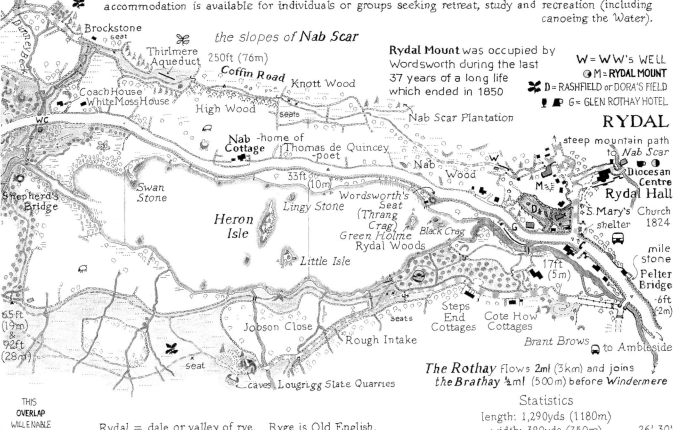

the slopes of **Nab Scar**

Rydal Mount was occupied by Wordsworth during the last 37 years of a long life which ended in 1850

W = WW's WELL
M = **RYDAL MOUNT**
D = RASHFIELD or DORA'S FIELD
G = GLEN ROTHAY HOTEL

Dunney Beck

Brockstone
seat

Thirlmere Aqueduct
250ft (76m)
Coffin Road
Knott Wood

Coach House
White Moss House

High Wood

seats

Nab Scar Plantation

RYDAL

steep mountain path to *Nab Scar*

WC

Nab -home of
Cottage Thomas de Quincey
-poet

Nab

Wood

Diocesan Centre
Rydal Hall

S. Mary's Church
shelter 1824

Shepherd's Bridge

Swan
Stone

33ft (10m)

Lingy Stone

Wordsworth's Seat
(Thrang Crag)

Green Holme

Black Crag

Rydal Woods

mile stone
Pelter Bridge
-6ft (-2m)

Heron Isle

Little Isle

65 ft (19m) &
92ft (28m)

seat

Jobson Close

Rough Intake

seats

Steps End Cottages

Cote How Cottages

Brant Brows to Ambleside

caves Loughrigg Slate Quarries

The Rothay flows 2ml (3km) and joins
the Brathay ½ml (500m) before *Windermere*

17ft (5m)

THIS
OVERLAP
WILL ENABLE
MOTORISTS
TO PARK,
USE THE **WC**,
THEN VISIT
EITHER LAKE

TAKE CARE
ON THE BUSY
HIGHWAY

Rydal = dale or valley of rye. Ryge is Old English.
Dale derives from Norse. Water is OE, in this sense, a lake.
An early name was ROUTHAMERE from the river.
The river name ROTHAY derives from the Old Norse
Rauth-á = Red-river The 'red one' is a literal form of trout.
Traditionally they adopt this stream on leaving Windermere,
whereas char ascend the Broad-river or Brathay.

2° 59' W

58' 30"

Statistics
length: 1,290yds (1180m)
width: 380yds (350m)
max depth 56ft (17m)
surface level 177ft (54m)
area: 0·12 sq mls (0·31sq km)

26' 30"

RYDAL WATER

Long 2° 58' W

Dividing Windermere and Elter Water from Grasmere and Rydal Water, Loughrigg is a craggy hill much favoured by walkers. Strongly recommended for a first ascent to active newcomers, its many tops give splendid views of these Lakes. Derived from the Irish-Gaelic *lough* - "lake", plus Norse *hyggr* - "rigg" or "ridge", this miniature mountain is appropriately named. The Loughrigg **Fell** on maps refers to one of five unenclosed old Parish Commons, which Lord Lonsdale leased to the National Trust forty years ago. Strictly, names of this genre indicate tracts of land defined by usage and stewardship rather than natural hills and mountains lying within or straddling their boundaries.

GRASMERE and RYDAL WATER lie in the prettiest, if busiest, vale. Forever associated with Wordsworth and the Lake Poets who chose to make their homes here, the area is a lodestar for the international traveller and literary specialist. Grasmere's Sports began in 1868 and continue to attract visitors and locals to traditional events and competitions. Non-motorised boats may be launched on Grasmere from the landings at "Allonbys" for a fee. Only private rights of boating exist for Rydal Water.

ELTER WATER, smaller even than Brothers Water, completes a trio of tiny lakes. Here, Beatrix Potter depicted her amphibious character, Jeremy Fisher. The intimacy of these pretty sheets of water is greatly appreciated by the artist. Main roads and some of Lakeland's most popular paths hug the best-known shores in the Lake District. Everyone can enjoy their beauties at close call. Motorists get to see these tiny jewels from Wishing Gate lane and Red Bank. The paths by Elter Water are sections of a long-distance route, the "Cumbria Way".

ESTHWAITE WATER and CONISTON WATER are situated in the old County of Lancashire's Over-Sands, Furness area. Esthwaite Water primarily caters for the fisherman and others who enjoy quiet contemplation. Another Beatrix Potter Tale, that involving Mr. Tod, is set by these waters. During summer a bus service provides a tenuous link with the Windermere Ferry. In contrast the old capital Hawkshead, with its mediæval alleys such as "Leather, Rag and Putty Street" (re-named Wordsworth Street), is extremely busy but can, with some justice, claim to be the prettiest village in Lakeland.

Over the hills, beyond the beauty-spot of Tarn Hows, lie the Coniston Fells providing a noble backdrop for the lake once known as Thorstein's Mere. Thursteinn or Thorstein was a Norse coloniser. The current appellation identifies with the rather more workaday but accommodating village of Coniston - the "King's Farm". Coningeston was a 12th Century spelling. "Konyngr" or "Cyningk" is Norse or Old English for king while "tun" is an Old English word which originally signified hedge, then the farm or house it enclosed and finally the settlement. "Wastre" is the Old English water, in the sense of a lake. The le Flemings came to Coniston Hall in the 13th Century and built an impressive mansion in the 15th before moving on to Rydal Hall. Its camp-site occupies a perfect base for small-boat users. Alfred Lord Tennyson, Poet Laureate, honeymooned at Tent Lodge on the eastern shore. John Ruskin declared the view from his home, Brantwood, "the Best in all England".

The railway took over the task of transporting copper and slate from the lake barges and also imported tourists. Its unaccountable demise took place in 1961. The steam yacht *Gondola* was launched in 1859, the year the railway came to the village, then ferried between Waterhead and Lake Bank Piers until she was de-commissioned in 1936. For nearly thirty years she lay in the reeds by Nibthwaite, serving as a houseboat until a storm sank her. Vickers of Barrow restored her for the National Trust, and since 1980 folk have been able to glide once more in upholstered comfort from the Boating Centre to Brantwood and the "Park-a-Moor" pier at Rigg Wood car park. Coniston Launch operate a complementary, if more comprehensive, ferry service between landing stages on both sides and either end of the lake. The season for both enterprises, which also offer special interest cruises, extends from the last weekend in March to the first in November. National Trust, National Park Authority and Forestry Commission properties permit exploration on foot and provide access to many parts of the shore. The "Cumbria Way" has popularised the western side. Coniston Water could be summarised as being very user-friendly. Every activity from scuba-diving to yacht racing, or motor-cruising to kayaking, can be observed most weekends by visitors relaxing or rambling on the shores of this accessible water.

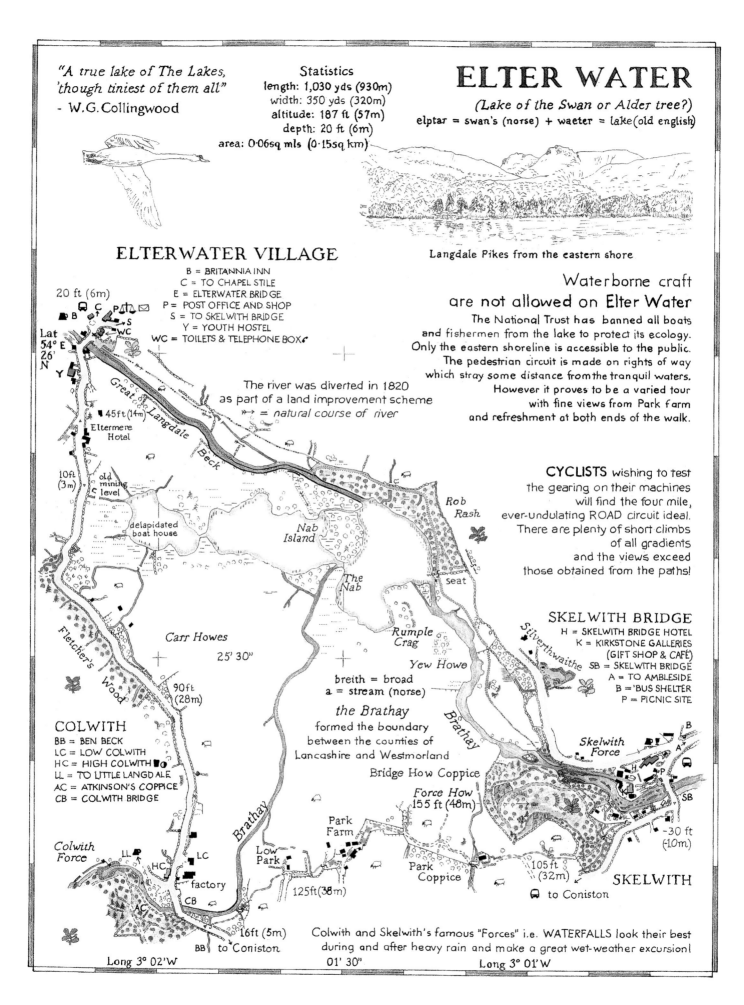

ELTER WATER
(Lake of the Swan or Alder tree?)
elptar = swan's (norse) + waeter = lake (old english)

"A true lake of The Lakes, 'though tiniest of them all" - W.G. Collingwood

Statistics
length: 1,030 yds (930m)
width: 350 yds (320m)
altitude: 187 ft (57m)
depth: 20 ft (6m)
area: 0·06 sq mls (0·155 sq km)

Langdale Pikes from the eastern shore.

ELTERWATER VILLAGE
B = BRITANNIA INN
C = TO CHAPEL STILE
E = ELTERWATER BRIDGE
P = POST OFFICE AND SHOP
S = TO SKELWITH BRIDGE
Y = YOUTH HOSTEL
WC = TOILETS & TELEPHONE BOX

20 ft (6m)

Lat 54° 26' N

Great Langdale Beck

The river was diverted in 1820 as part of a land improvement scheme
↠ = natural course of river

45ft (14m)
Eltermere Hotel

10ft (3m)
old mining level

delapidated boat house

Nab Island

The Nab

Rob Rash

seat

Waterborne craft are not allowed on Elter Water
The National Trust has banned all boats and fishermen from the lake to protect its ecology. Only the eastern shoreline is accessible to the public. The pedestrian circuit is made on rights of way which stray some distance from the tranquil waters. However it proves to be a varied tour with fine views from Park farm and refreshment at both ends of the walk.

CYCLISTS wishing to test the gearing on their machines will find the four mile, ever-undulating ROAD circuit ideal. There are plenty of short climbs of all gradients and the views exceed those obtained from the paths!

Fletcher's Wood

Carr Howes
25' 30"

90ft (28m)

Rumple Crag

Yew Howe

breith = broad
a = stream (norse)

the Brathay formed the boundary between the counties of Lancashire and Westmorland

COLWITH
BB = BEN BECK
LC = LOW COLWITH
HC = HIGH COLWITH
LL = TO LITTLE LANGDALE
AC = ATKINSON'S COPPICE
CB = COLWITH BRIDGE

Colwith Force
LL
HC
LC
factory
CB
AC

16ft (5m)
BB to Coniston

Brathay

Bridge How Coppice

Force How
155 ft (48m)

Park Farm
Low Park

Park Coppice

125ft (38m)

SKELWITH BRIDGE
H = SKELWITH BRIDGE HOTEL
K = KIRKSTONE GALLERIES (GIFT SHOP & CAFÉ)
SB = SKELWITH BRIDGE
A = TO AMBLESIDE
B = 'BUS SHELTER
P = PICNIC SITE

Silverthwaithe

Skelwith Force

Brathay

~30 ft (10m)

105 ft (32m)

SKELWITH
to Coniston

Colwith and Skelwith's famous "Forces" i.e. WATERFALLS look their best during and after heavy rain and make a great wet-weather excursion!

Long 3° 02'W   01' 30"   Long 3° 01'W

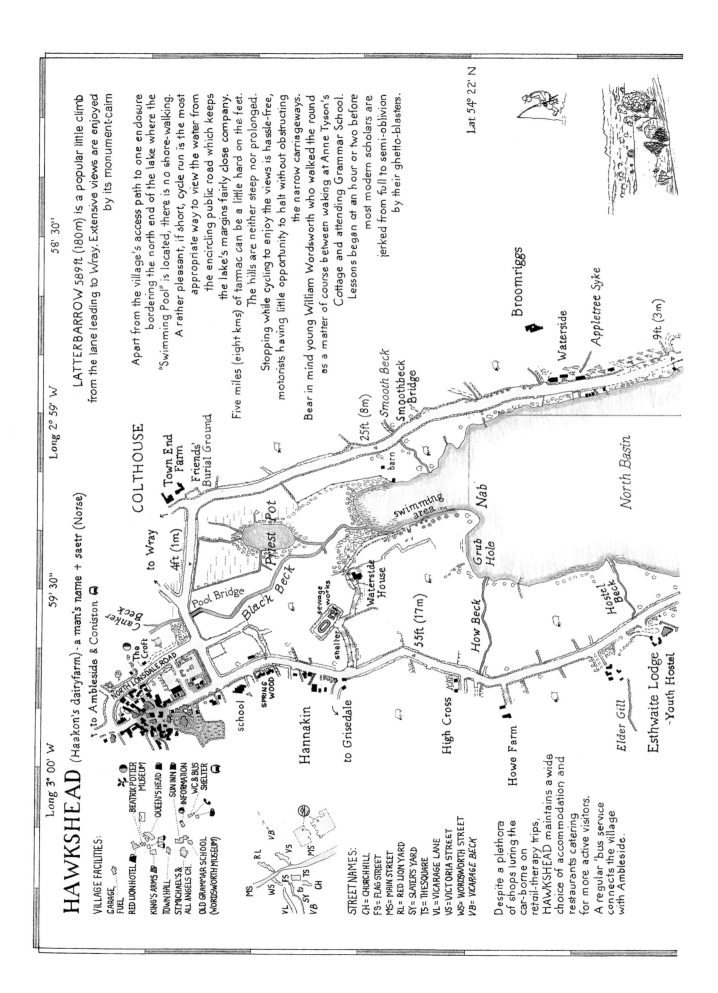

HAWKSHEAD (Haakon's dairyfarm) - a man's name + saetr (Norse)

VILLAGE FACILITIES:

GARAGE
FUEL
RED LION HOTEL
KING'S ARMS
TOWN HALL
ST. MICHAEL'S & ALL ANGELS CH.
OLD GRAMMAR SCHOOL (WORDSWORTH MUSEUM)
BEATRIX POTTER MUSEUM
QUEEN'S HEAD
SUN INN
INFORMATION
WC & BUS SHELTER

STREET NAMES:

CH = CHURCH HILL
FS = FLAG STREET
MS = MAIN STREET
RL = RED LION YARD
SY = SLATER'S YARD
TS = THE SQUARE
VL = VICARAGE LANE
VS = VICTORIA STREET
WS = WORDSWORTH STREET
VB = VICARAGE BECK

Despite a plethora of shops luring the car-borne on retail-therapy trips, HAWKSHEAD maintains a wide choice of accommodation and restaurants catering for more active visitors.

A regular 'bus service connects the village with Ambleside.

LATTERBARROW 589ft (180m) is a popular little climb from the lane leading to Wray. Extensive views are enjoyed by its monument-cairn.

Apart from the village's access path to one enclosure bordering the north end of the lake where the "Swimming Pool" is located, there is no shore-walking.

A rather pleasant, if short, cycle run is the most appropriate way to view the water from the encircling public road which keeps the lake's margins fairly close company.

Five miles (eight kms) of tarmac can be a little hard on the feet. The hills are neither steep nor prolonged.

Stopping while cycling to enjoy the views is hassle-free, motorists having little opportunity to halt without obstructing the narrow carriageways.

Bear in mind young William Wordsworth who walked the round as a matter of course between waking at Anne Tyson's Cottage and attending Grammar School.

Lessons began at an hour or two before most modern scholars are jerked from full to semi-oblivion by their ghetto-blasters.

Map labels: to Ambleside & Coniston · NORTH LONSDALE ROAD · The Croft · Canter Beck · to Wray · COLTHOUSE · Town End Farm · Friends' Burial Ground · Pool Bridge · Black Beck · Priest Pot · 4ft (1m) · school · SPRING WOOD · Hannakin · to Grisedale · sewage works · shelter · Waterside House · swimming area · 25ft (8m) · Smooth Beck · Smoothbeck Bridge · barn · Nab · Grub Hole · North Bastin · Broomriggs · Waterside · Appletree Syke · 9ft (3m) · How Beck · Hostel Beck · 55ft (17m) · High Cross · Howe Farm · Elder Gill · Esthwaite Lodge ~Youth Hostel

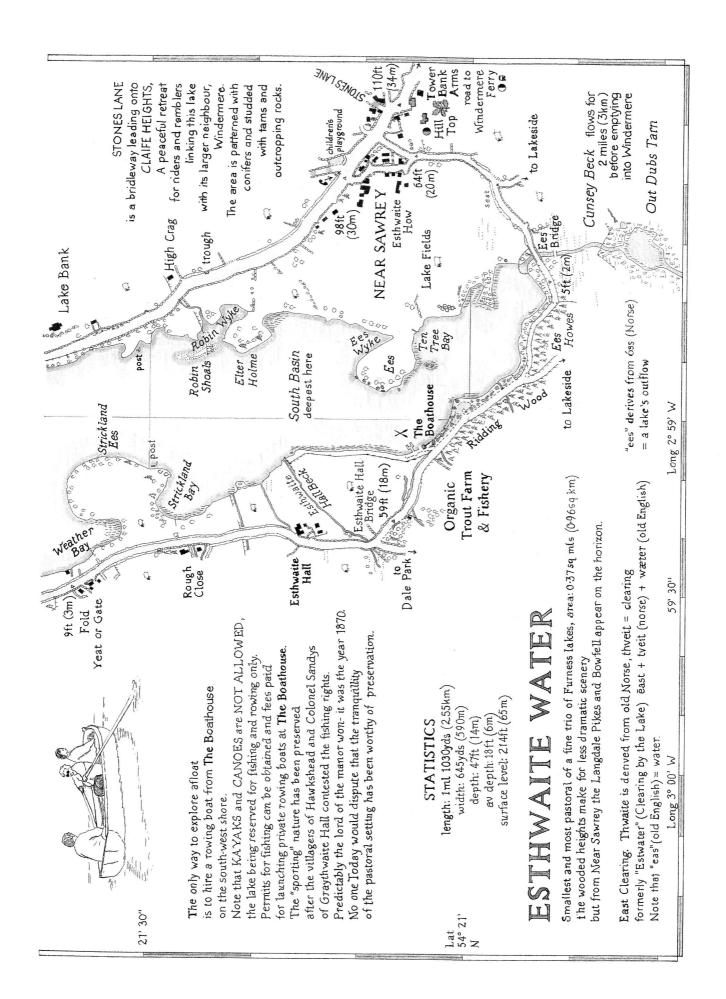

ESTHWAITE WATER

Smallest and most pastoral of a fine trio of Furness lakes, area: 0·37 sq mls (0·96 sq km). the wooded heights make for less dramatic scenery but from Near Sawrey the Langdale Pikes and Bowfell appear on the horizon.

East Clearing. Thwaite is derived from old Norse, thveit = clearing formerly "Estwater" (Clearing by the Lake) ēast + tveit (norse) + wæter (old English) Note that "eas"(old English) = water.

STATISTICS

length: 1ml 1030yds (2·55km)
width: 645yds (590m)
depth: 47ft (14m)
av depth: 18ft (6m)
surface level: 214ft (65m)

The only way to explore afloat is to hire a rowing boat from **The Boathouse** on the south-west shore.
Note that KAYAKS and CANOES are NOT ALLOWED, the lake being reserved for fishing and rowing only. Permits for fishing can be obtained and fees paid for launching private rowing boats at **The Boathouse.**
The "sporting" nature has been preserved after the villages of Hawkshead and Colonel Sandys of Graythwaite Hall contested the fishing rights. Predictably the lord of the manor won - it was the year 1870. No one Today would dispute that the tranquillity of the pastoral setting has been worthy of preservation.

STONES LANE is a bridleway leading onto CLAIFE HEIGHTS, A peaceful retreat for riders and ramblers linking this lake with its larger neighbour, Windermere. The area is patterned with conifers and studded with tarns and outcropping rocks.

Lat 54° 21' N

Long 3° 00' W

21' 30"

59' 30"

Long 2° 59' W

"ees" derives from óss (Norse) = a lake's outflow

Lake Bank

High Crag

trough

STONES LANE

110ft (34m)

Tower Bank Arms

Hill Top

children's playground

road to Windermere Ferry

98ft (30m)

Esthwaite How

64ft (20m)

NEAR SAWREY

Lake Fields

to Lakeside

Cunsey Beck flows for 2 miles (3km) before emptying into Windermere

Out Dubs Tarn

post

Robin Wyke

Robin Shoals

Elter Holme

South Basin deepest here

Ees Wyke

Ees

Ees

Ten Tree Bay

seat

Ees Bridge

5ft (2m)

Ees Howes

Strickland Ees

post

Strickland Bay

The Boathouse

Ridding Wood

to Lakeside

Weather Bay

9ft (3m) Fold Yeat or Gate

Rough Close

Esthwaite Hall

Esthwaite Hall Beck

Esthwaite Hall Bridge

59ft (18m)

Organic Trout Farm & Fishery

to Dale Park

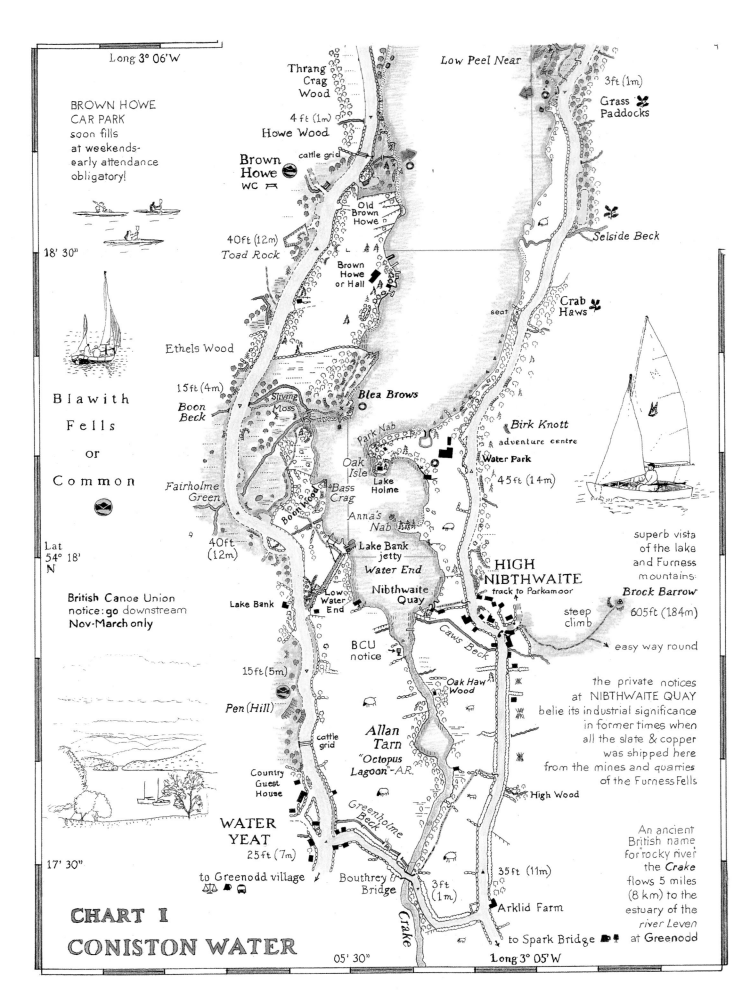

Long 3° 06'W

BROWN HOWE
CAR PARK
soon fills
at weekends-
early attendance
obligatory!

18' 30"

B l a w i t h

F e l l s

o r

C o m m o n

Lat
54° 18'
N

British Canoe Union
notice: go downstream
Nov-March only

17' 30"

Thrang
Crag
Wood

Low Peel Near

3ft (1m)

Grass
Paddocks

4 ft (1m)
Howe Wood

cattle grid

BROWN
HOWE
WC

Old
Brown
Howe

Selside Beck

40ft (12m)
Toad Rock

Brown
Howe
or Hall

seat

Crab
Haws

Ethels Wood

15ft (4m)

Sliving
Moss

Blea Brows

Birk Knott

Boon
Beck

adventure centre

Park Nab

Water Park

Oak
Isle

45ft (14m)

Fairholme
Green

Bass
Crag

Lake
Holme

Boon
Wood

Anna's
Nab

superb vista
of the lake
and Furness
mountains

40ft
(12m)

Lake Bank
jetty

Water End

HIGH
NIBTHWAITE

Brock Barrow

track to Parkamoor

605ft (184m)

Lake Bank

Low
Water
End

Nibthwaite
Quay

steep
climb

easy way round

15ft (5m)

BCU
notice

Caws Beck

the private notices
at NIBTHWAITE QUAY
belie its industrial significance
in former times when
all the slate & copper
was shipped here
from the mines and quarries
of the Furness Fells

Pen (Hill)

Oak Haw
Wood

Allan
Tarn
"Octopus
Lagoon"-AR.

cattle
grid

Country
Guest
House

High Wood

Greenholme
Beck

An ancient
British name
for rocky river
the Crake
flows 5 miles
(8 km) to the
estuary of the
river Leven
at Greenodd

WATER
YEAT

25ft (7m)

to Greenodd village

Bouthrey
Bridge

3ft
(1m)

35ft (11m)

Arklid Farm

Crake

to Spark Bridge

Long 3° 05'W

05' 30"

CHART I
CONISTON WATER

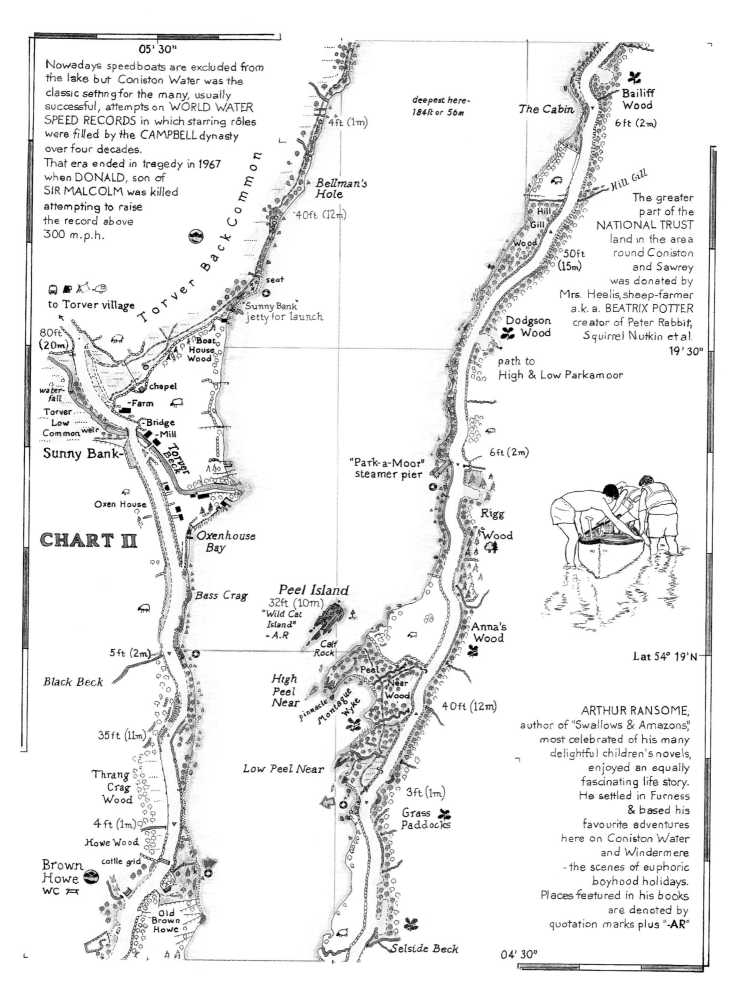

Nowadays speedboats are excluded from the lake but Coniston Water was the classic setting for the many, usually successful, attempts on WORLD WATER SPEED RECORDS in which starring rôles were filled by the CAMPBELL dynasty over four decades.

That era ended in tragedy in 1967 when DONALD, son of SIR MALCOLM was killed attempting to raise the record above 300 m.p.h.

to Torver village

80ft (20m)

waterfall

Torver Low Common

weir

Sunny Bank-

Oxen House

CHART II

Bass Crag

5 ft (2m)

Black Beck

35 ft (11m)

Thrang Crag Wood

4 ft (1m)

Howe Wood

cattle grid

Brown Howe

WC

Old Brown Howe

Torver Back Common

Bellman's Hole

40ft (12m)

seat

Sunny Bank" jetty for launch

Boat House Wood

chapel

-Farm

-Bridge

-Mill

Torver Beck

Oxenhouse Bay

Peel Island
32ft (10m)
"Wild Cat Island"
- A.R

Calf Rock

High Peel Near

Pinnacle

Montague Wyke

Peel

Near Wood

Low Peel Near

4 ft (1m)

deepest here- 184ft or 56m

The Cabin

Bailiff Wood
6 ft (2m)

Hill Gill

Hill Gill Wood

50ft (15m)

The greater part of the NATIONAL TRUST land in the area round Coniston and Sawrey was donated by Mrs. Heelis, sheep-farmer a.k.a. BEATRIX POTTER creator of Peter Rabbit, Squirrel Nutkin et al.

Dodgson Wood

path to High & Low Parkamoor

6 ft (2m)

"Park-a-Moor" steamer pier

Rigg Wood

Anna's Wood

40 ft (12m)

3ft (1m)

Grass Paddocks

Selside Beck

Lat 54° 19'N

ARTHUR RANSOME, author of "Swallows & Amazons", most celebrated of his many delightful children's novels, enjoyed an equally fascinating life story. He settled in Furness & based his favourite adventures here on Coniston Water and Windermere - the scenes of euphoric boyhood holidays. Places featured in his books are denoted by quotation marks plus "-AR"

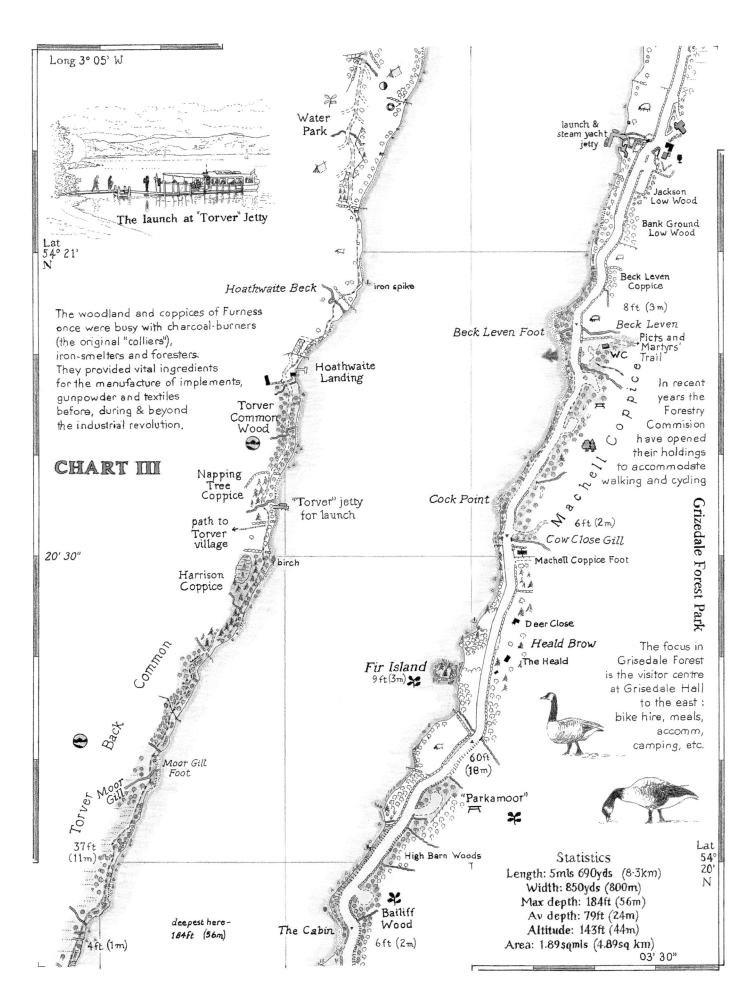

Long 3° 05' W

The launch at "Torver" Jetty

Lat
54° 21'
N

Water
Park

Hoathwaite Beck

iron spike

The woodland and coppices of Furness
once were busy with charcoal-burners
(the original "colliers"),
iron-smelters and foresters.
They provided vital ingredients
for the manufacture of implements,
gunpowder and textiles
before, during & beyond
the industrial revolution.

CHART III

20' 30"

Hoathwaite
Landing

Torver
Common
Wood

Napping
Tree
Coppice

"Torver" jetty
for launch

path to
Torver
village

birch

Harrison
Coppice

Back

Common

Moor Gill
Foot

Torver Moor
Gill

37ft
(11m)

deepest here –
184ft (56m)

4ft (1m)

The Cabin

Bailiff
Wood

6ft (2m)

High Barn Woods

Fir Island
9ft (3m)

60ft
(18m)

"Parkamoor"

launch &
steam yacht
jetty

Jackson
Low Wood

Bank Ground
Low Wood

Beck Leven
Coppice

8ft (3m)

Beck Leven Foot

Beck Leven
Picts and
Martyrs'
Trail

WC

Machell Coppice

In recent
years the
Forestry
Commision
have opened
their holdings
to accommodate
walking and cycling

Cock Point

6ft (2m)

Cow Close Gill

Machell Coppice Foot

Deer Close

Heald Brow

The Heald

Grizedale Forest Park

The focus in
Grisedale Forest
is the visitor centre
at Grisedale Hall
to the east :
bike hire, meals,
accomm,
camping, etc.

Lat
54°
20'
N

Statistics
Length: 5mls 690yds (8·3km)
Width: 850yds (800m)
Max depth: 184ft (56m)
Av depth: 79ft (24m)
Altitude: 143ft (44m)
Area: 1.89 sqmls (4.89 sq km)

03' 30"

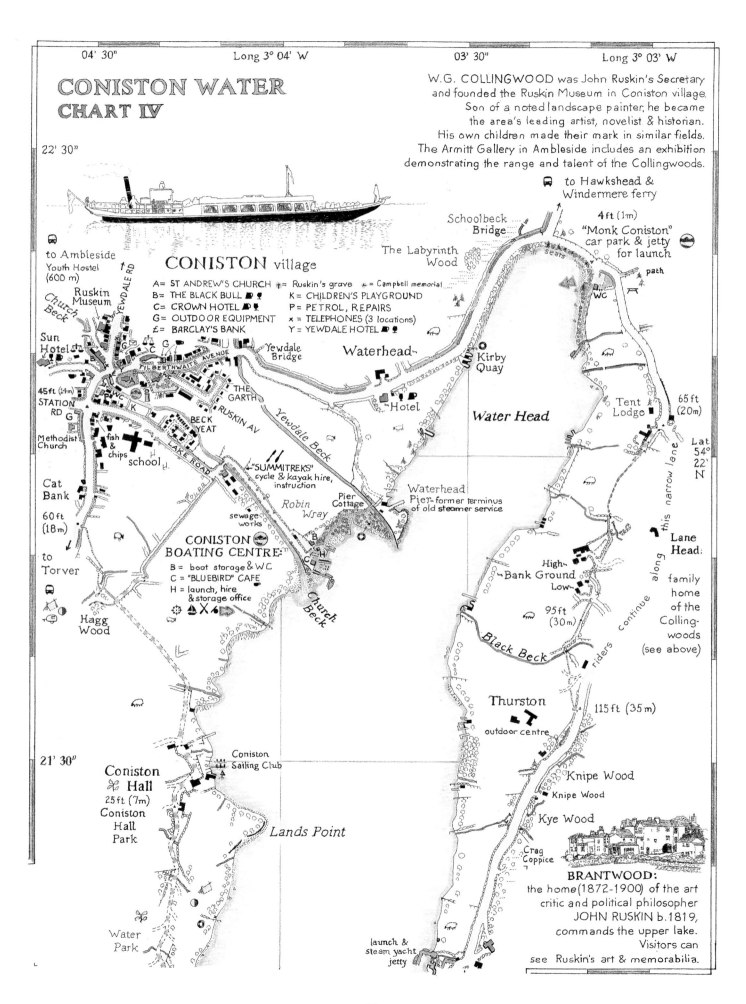

CONISTON WATER CHART IV

W.G. COLLINGWOOD was John Ruskin's Secretary and founded the Ruskin Museum in Coniston village. Son of a noted landscape painter, he became the area's leading artist, novelist & historian. His own children made their mark in similar fields. The Armitt Gallery in Ambleside includes an exhibition demonstrating the range and talent of the Collingwoods.

22' 30"

to Hawkshead & Windermere ferry

4 ft (1m)

Schoolbeck Bridge

"Monk Coniston" car park & jetty for launch

The Labyrinth Wood

WC path seats

to Ambleside
Youth Hostel (600 m)

CONISTON village

A = ST ANDREW'S CHURCH   ‡ = Ruskin's grave   ⚑ = Campbell memorial
B = THE BLACK BULL   K = CHILDREN'S PLAYGROUND
C = CROWN HOTEL   P = PETROL, REPAIRS
G = OUTDOOR EQUIPMENT   x = TELEPHONES (3 locations)
£ = BARCLAY'S BANK   Y = YEWDALE HOTEL

Ruskin Museum

Church Beck

Sun Hotel

Yewdale Bridge

Waterhead

Kirby Quay

Tent Lodge

65 ft (20m)

45ft (14m)
STATION RD

THE GARTH

Water Head

Lat 54° 22' N

Methodist Church

fish & chips

BECK YEAT

school

RUSKIN AV

Yewdale Beck

Cat Bank

60 ft (18m)

"SUMMITREKS" cycle & kayak hire, instruction

Robin Wray

Pier Cottage

Waterhead Pier- former terminus of old steamer service

Lane Head:

family home of the Colling-woods (see above)

to Torver

sewage works

CONISTON BOATING CENTRE:
B = boat storage & WC
C = "BLUEBIRD" CAFE
H = launch, hire & storage office

High-
Bank Ground
Low

95 ft (30m)

Hagg Wood

Church Beck

Black Beck

riders continue along this narrow lane

Thurston

outdoor centre

115 ft (35m)

Coniston Sailing Club

Knipe Wood

21' 30"

Coniston Hall

25 ft (7m)

Coniston Hall Park

Knipe Wood

Kye Wood

Crag Coppice

Lands Point

BRANTWOOD:
the home (1872-1900) of the art critic and political philosopher JOHN RUSKIN b.1819, commands the upper lake. Visitors can see Ruskin's art & memorabilia.

Water Park

launch & steam yacht jetty

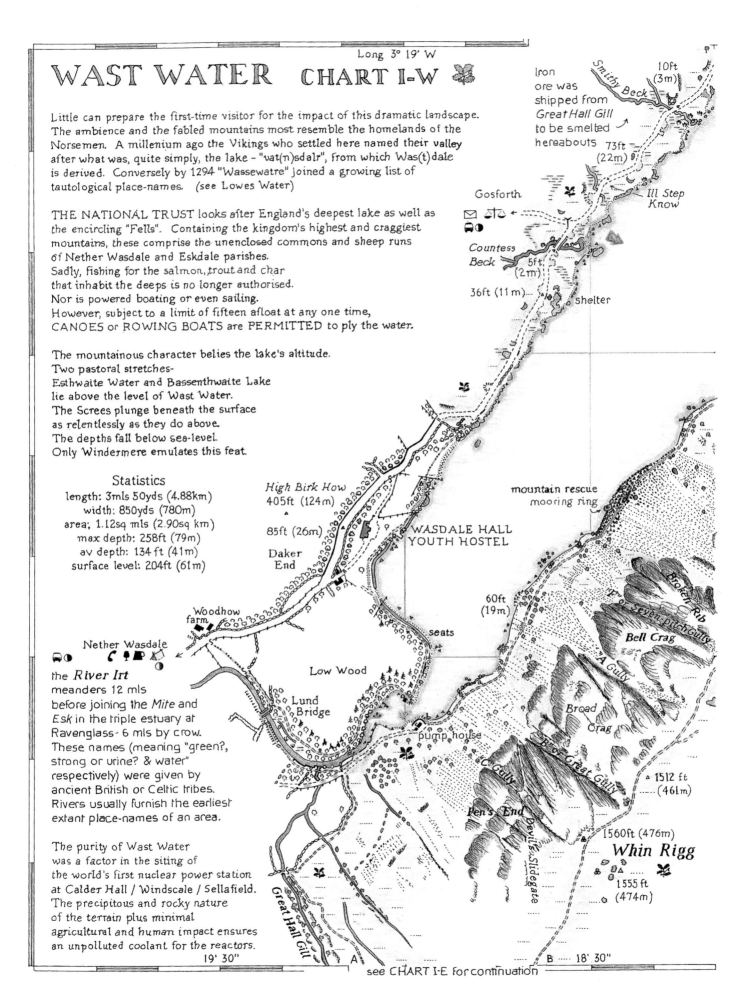

WAST WATER CHART I-W

Long 3° 19' W

Little can prepare the first-time visitor for the impact of this dramatic landscape. The ambience and the fabled mountains most resemble the homelands of the Norsemen. A millenium ago the Vikings who settled here named their valley after what was, quite simply, the lake – "vat(n)sdalr", from which Was(t)dale is derived. Conversely by 1294 "Wassewatre" joined a growing list of tautological place-names. (see Lowes Water)

THE NATIONAL TRUST looks after England's deepest lake as well as the encircling "Fells". Containing the kingdom's highest and craggiest mountains, these comprise the unenclosed commons and sheep runs of Nether Wasdale and Eskdale parishes.
Sadly, fishing for the salmon, trout and char that inhabit the deeps is no longer authorised.
Nor is powered boating or even sailing.
However, subject to a limit of fifteen afloat at any one time, CANOES or ROWING BOATS are PERMITTED to ply the water.

The mountainous character belies the lake's altitude.
Two pastoral stretches-
Esthwaite Water and Bassenthwaite Lake
lie above the level of Wast Water.
The Screes plunge beneath the surface
as relentlessly as they do above.
The depths fall below sea-level.
Only Windermere emulates this feat.

Statistics
length: 3mls 50yds (4.88km)
width: 850yds (780m)
area: 1.12sq mls (2.90sq km)
max depth: 258ft (79m)
av depth: 134 ft (41m)
surface level: 204ft (61m)

the *River Irt*
meanders 12 mls
before joining the *Mite* and
Esk in the triple estuary at
Ravenglass- 6 mls by crow.
These names (meaning "green?,
strong or urine? & water"
respectively) were given by
ancient British or Celtic tribes.
Rivers usually furnish the earliest
extant place-names of an area.

The purity of Wast Water
was a factor in the siting of
the world's first nuclear power station
at Calder Hall / Windscale / Sellafield.
The precipitous and rocky nature
of the terrain plus minimal
agricultural and human impact ensures
an unpolluted coolant for the reactors.
19' 30"

Iron ore was shipped from *Great Hall Gill* to be smelted hereabouts

Smithy Beck
10ft (3m)
73ft (22m)
Ill Step Know

Gosforth

Countess Beck
5ft (2m)
36ft (11m)
shelter

High Birk How
405ft (124m)
85ft (26m)
Daker End

mountain rescue mooring ring

WASDALE HALL YOUTH HOSTEL

60ft (19m)

seats

Woodhow farm

Nether Wasdale

Low Wood

Lund Bridge

pump house

Broken Rib
Seven Pitch Gully
Bell Crag
"A" Gully
Broad Crag
"B" or Great Gully
1512 ft (461m)
"C" Gully
Pen's End
Devil's Slidegate
1560ft (476m)
Whin Rigg
1555 ft (474m)

Great Hall Gill

A
B --- 18' 30"

see CHART I-E for continuation

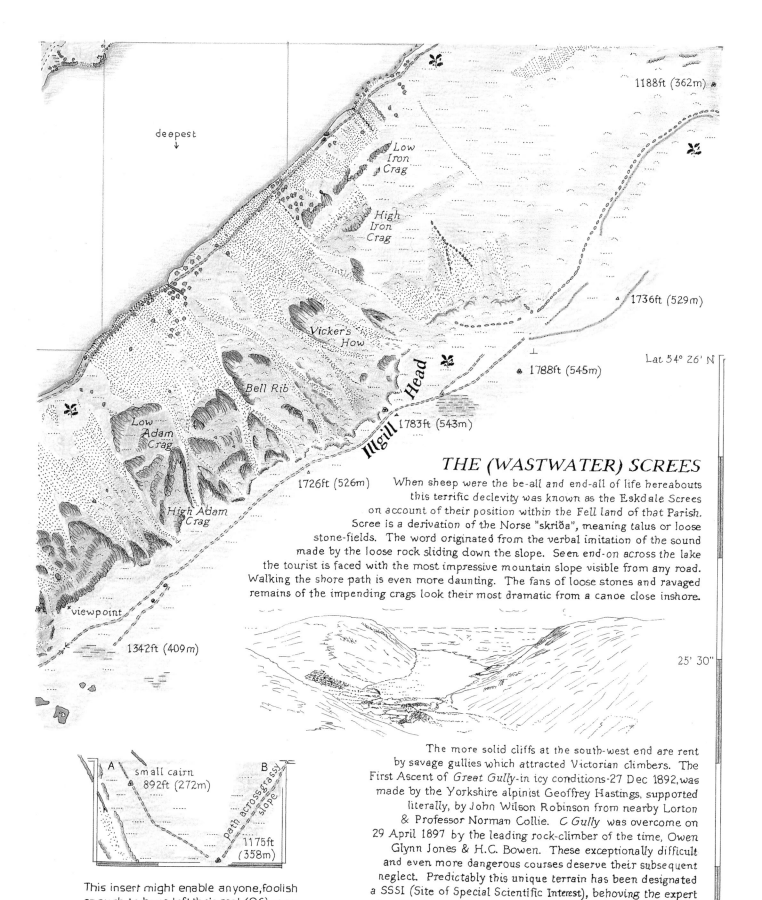

deepest
↓

1188ft (362m)

Low
Iron
Crag

High
Iron
Crag

1736ft (529m)

Vicker's
How

Lat 54° 26' N

1788ft (545m)

Bell Rib

Illgill Head

1783ft (543m)

Low
Adam
Crag

THE (WASTWATER) SCREES

1726ft (526m)

When sheep were the be-all and end-all of life hereabouts
this terrific declevity was known as the Eskdale Screes
on account of their position within the Fell land of that Parish.
Scree is a derivation of the Norse "skriða", meaning talus or loose
stone-fields. The word originated from the verbal imitation of the sound
made by the loose rock sliding down the slope. Seen end-on across the lake
the tourist is faced with the most impressive mountain slope visible from any road.
Walking the shore path is even more daunting. The fans of loose stones and ravaged
remains of the impending crags look their most dramatic from a canoe close inshore.

High Adam
Crag

viewpoint

1342ft (409m)

25' 30"

A small cairn
892ft (272m)

B

path across grassy
slope

1175ft
(358m)

The more solid cliffs at the south-west end are rent
by savage gullies which attracted Victorian climbers. The
First Ascent of *Great Gully* in icy conditions-27 Dec 1892, was
made by the Yorkshire alpinist Geoffrey Hastings, supported
literally, by John Wilson Robinson from nearby Lorton
& Professor Norman Collie. *C Gully* was overcome on
29 April 1897 by the leading rock-climber of the time, Owen
Glynn Jones & H.C. Bowen. These exceptionally difficult
and even more dangerous courses deserve their subsequent
neglect. Predictably this unique terrain has been designated
a SSSI (Site of Special Scientific Interest), behoving the expert
or inept to leave this untamed spot to nature and the naturalist.

This insert might enable anyone, foolish
enough to have left their real (OS) map
at base, to navigate over The Screes.

CHART I-E

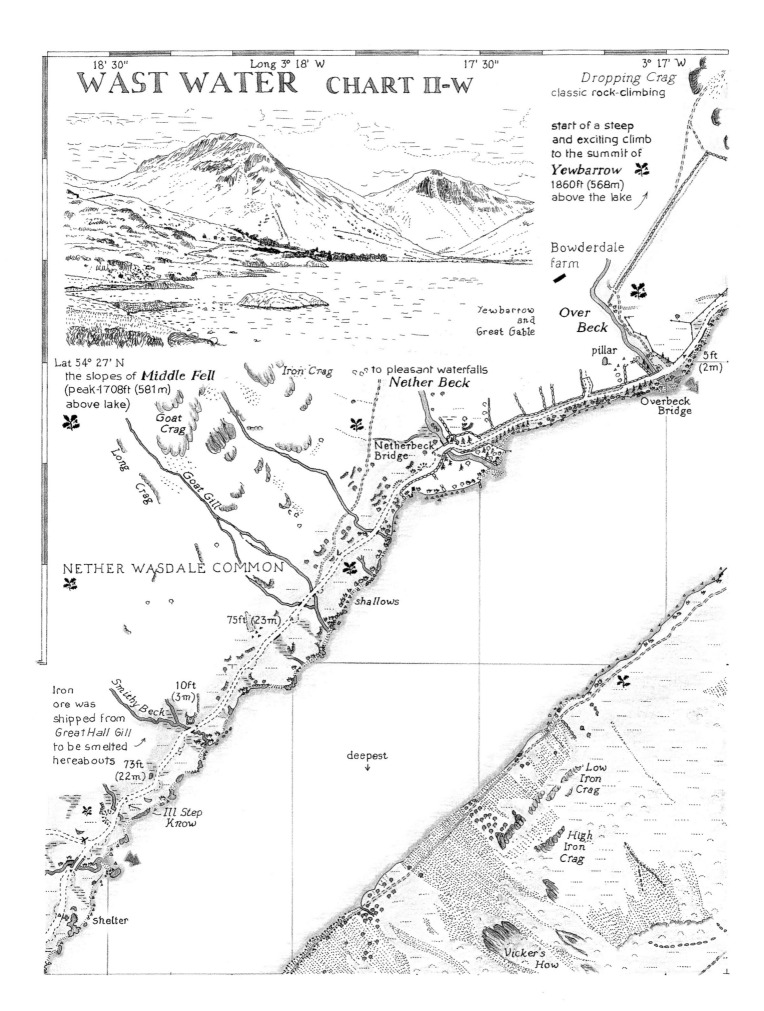

18' 30"

17' 30"

3° 17' W

WAST WATER CHART II-W

Dropping Crag
classic rock-climbing

start of a steep
and exciting climb
to the summit of
Yewbarrow 🌿
1860ft (568m)
above the lake ↑

Bowderdale
farm

Over
Beck

Yewbarrow
and
Great Gable

pillar

5 ft
(2m)

Lat 54° 27' N
the slopes of ***Middle Fell***
(peak 1708ft (581m)
above lake)

Iron Crag

to pleasant waterfalls
Nether Beck

Overbeck
Bridge

Goat
Crag

Netherbeck
Bridge

Long
Crag

Goat Gill

NETHER WASDALE COMMON

shallows

75ft (23m)

Iron
ore was
shipped from
Great Hall Gill
to be smelted
hereabouts

Smithy Beck

10ft
(3m)

deepest
↓

Low
Iron
Crag

73ft
(22m)

Ill Step
Know

High
Iron
Crag

shelter

Vicker's
How

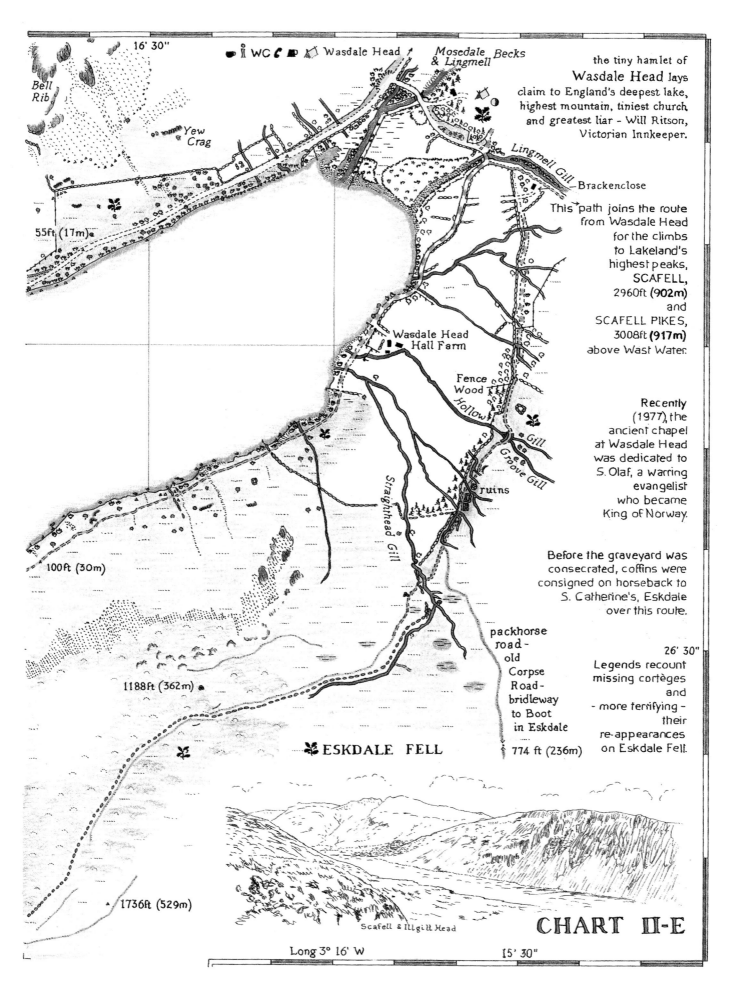

16' 30"

Bell Rib

🍺 ⅱ WC 🥾 🅿 🏠 Wasdale Head ↗   *Mosedale* Becks & *Lingmell*

Yew Crag

Lingmell Gill

Brackenclose

55ft (17m)

Wasdale Head Hall Farm

Fence Wood *Hollow*

Gill

Groove Gill

ruins

100ft (30m)

Straighthead Gill

1188ft (362m)

packhorse road - old Corpse Road - bridleway to Boot in Eskdale

🌸 ESKDALE FELL

774 ft (236m)

1736ft (529m)

Scafell & Illgill Head

Long 3° 16' W

15' 30"

the tiny hamlet of **Wasdale Head** lays claim to England's deepest lake, highest mountain, tiniest church and greatest liar - Will Ritson, Victorian Innkeeper.

This path joins the route from Wasdale Head for the climbs to Lakeland's highest peaks, SCAFELL, 2960ft **(902m)** and SCAFELL PIKES, 3008ft **(917m)** above Wast Water.

Recently (1977), the ancient chapel at Wasdale Head was dedicated to S. Olaf, a warring evangelist who became King of Norway.

Before the graveyard was consecrated, coffins were consigned on horseback to S. Catherine's, Eskdale over this route.

26' 30"

Legends recount missing cortèges and - more terrifying - their re-appearances on Eskdale Fell.

CHART II-E

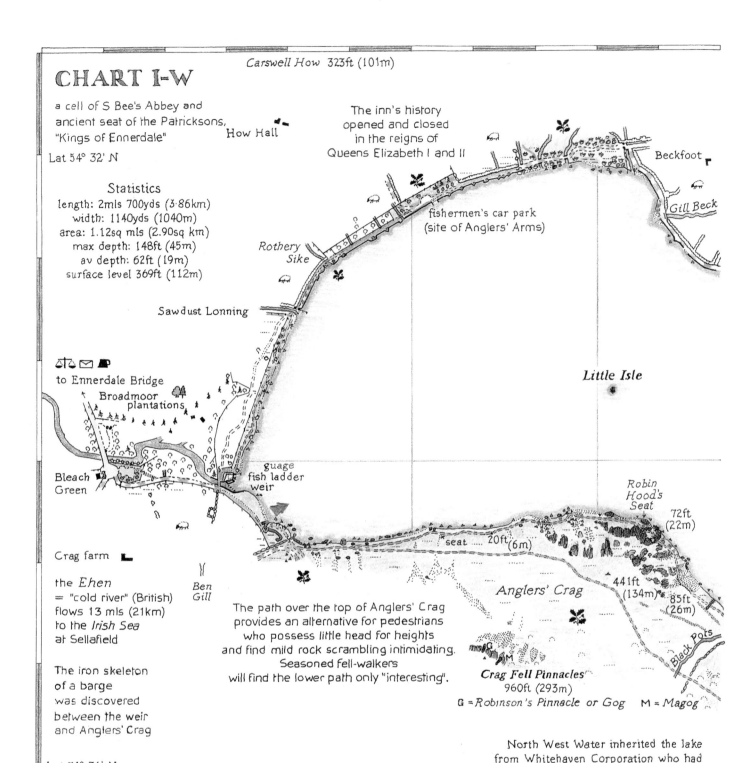

Carswell How 323ft (101m)

CHART I-W

a cell of S Bee's Abbey and
ancient seat of the Patricksons,
"Kings of Ennerdale"

Lat 54° 32' N

Statistics
length: 2mls 700yds (3·86km)
width: 1140yds (1040m)
area: 1.12sq mls (2.90sq km)
max depth: 148ft (45m)
av depth: 62ft (19m)
surface level 369ft (112m)

How Hall

The inn's history
opened and closed
in the reigns of
Queens Elizabeth I and II

Beckfoot

Gill Beck

fishermen's car park
(site of Anglers' Arms)

Rothery
Sike

Sawdust Lonning

to Ennerdale Bridge
Broadmoor
plantations

Little Isle

Bleach
Green

guage
fish ladder
weir

Robin
Hood's
Seat

72ft
(22m)

seat   20ft
(6m)

441ft
(134m)

85ft
(26m)

Crag farm

the *Ehen*
= "cold river" (British)
flows 13 mls (21km)
to the *Irish Sea*
at Sellafield

The iron skeleton
of a barge
was discovered
between the weir
and Anglers' Crag

Ben
Gill

The path over the top of Anglers' Crag
provides an alternative for pedestrians
who possess little head for heights
and find mild rock scrambling intimidating.
Seasoned fell-walkers
will find the lower path only "interesting".

Anglers' Crag

Black Pots

Crag Fell Pinnacles
960ft (293m)
G = Robinson's Pinnacle or Gog   M = Magog

Lat 54° 31' N

"Enner" might betoken a personal name,
Anander or Eghnar (Old English or Norse).
However it is generally accepted this element
is derived from the name for the outflow (see above),
"-dale" derives from Dalr (Norse) = valley,
"Water" from Vatn (Old English) = lake.
Thus *Ehen-dalr Vatn* means Cold river-valley Lake!

Old maps sometimes entitle the lake *Broad Water*.

North West Water inherited the lake
from Whitehaven Corporation who had
raised the level several feet since 1885.
Recent modernisation of the water
extraction and treatment plants has allowed
resumption of the issue of permits for boating

Fishing for the trout and char
is regulated by local angling associations.

A relict of the ice ages was a tiny marine shrimp
marooned by glacial action which,
adapted to the fresh water of
Ennerdale, was unique to Britain,
then became extinct in recent years.

North
West
Water
ENNERDALE WATER

24' 30"   Long 3° 24' W   23 30"

ACCESS PERMITS to LAUNCH/PUT-IN small, non-motorised CRAFT  CHART I-E
must be obtained in advance by writing to NWW, stating your planned
activity and date(s). Motor transport must be stationed in the public
parking areas and boats carried or propelled to shore manually:
(150 or 350 yard/metres portage at Bow Ness or between
Bleach Green and the weir). Swimming is prohibited.

North West Water Ltd
Northern Estates Office
The Old Sawmill, Thirlmere
KESWICK, Cumbria
CA12 4TQ

Lat 54° 32' N

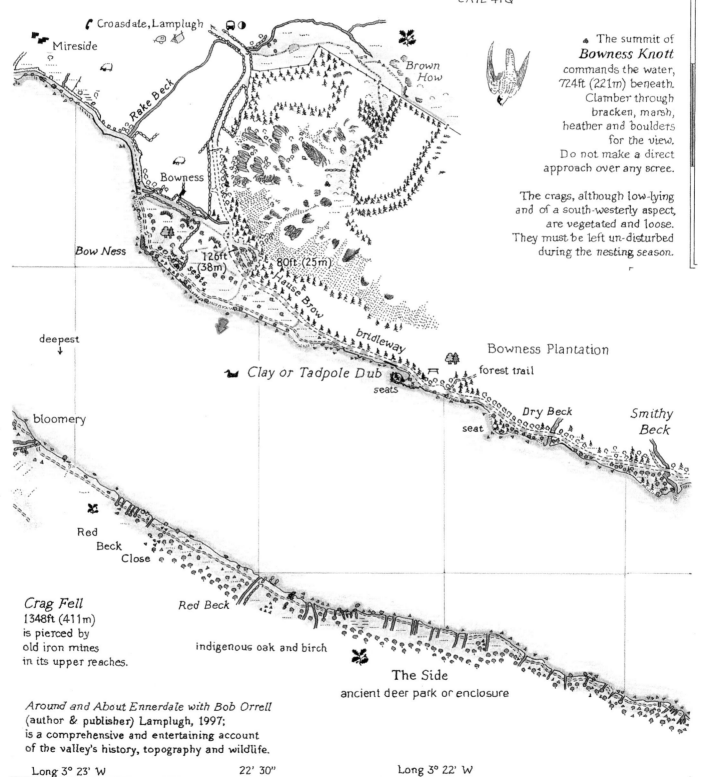

Croasdate, Lamplugh

Mireside

Rake Beck

Bowness

Bow Ness

126ft (38m)

80ft (25m)

Hause Brow

seats

deepest

bridleway

Clay or Tadpole Dub

seats

bloomery

Red Beck Close

Crag Fell
1348ft (411m)
is pierced by
old iron mines
in its upper reaches.

Red Beck

indigenous oak and birch

The Side
ancient deer park or enclosure

Brown How

The summit of
Bowness Knott
commands the water,
724ft (221m) beneath.
Clamber through
bracken, marsh,
heather and boulders
for the view.
Do not make a direct
approach over any scree.

The crags, although low-lying
and of a south-westerly aspect,
are vegetated and loose.
They must be left un-disturbed
during the nesting season.

Bowness Plantation
forest trail

seat

Dry Beck

Smithy Beck

Around and About Ennerdale with Bob Orrell
(author & publisher) Lamplugh, 1997;
is a comprehensive and entertaining account
of the valley's history, topography and wildlife.

Long 3° 23' W   22' 30"   Long 3° 22' W

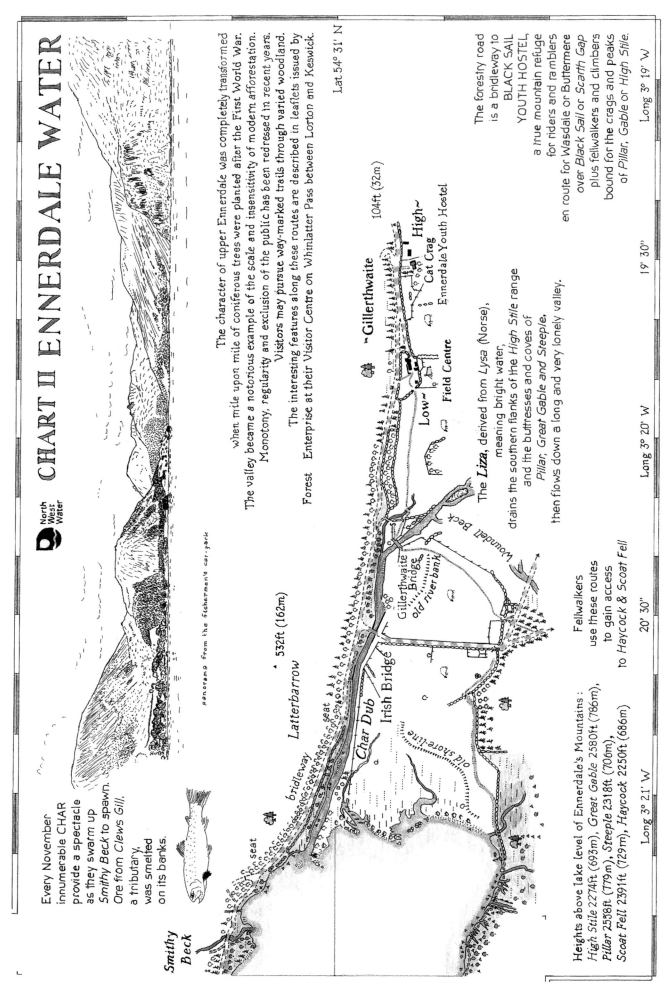

CHART II ENNERDALE WATER

North West Water

The character of upper Ennerdale was completely transformed when mile upon mile of coniferous trees were planted after the First World War. The valley became a notorious example of the scale and insensitivity of modern afforestation. Monotony, regularity and exclusion of the public has been redressed in recent years. Visitors may pursue way-marked trails through varied woodland.

The interesting features along these routes are described in leaflets issued by Forest Enterprise at their Visitor Centre on Whinlatter Pass between Lorton and Keswick.

Lat 54° 31' N

Panorama from the fishermen's car-park

Smithy Beck

Every November innumerable CHAR provide a spectacle as they swarm up *Smithy Beck* to spawn. Ore from *Clews Gill*, a tributary, was smelted on its banks.

▲ 532ft (162m)
Latterbarrow

seat

bridleway

Char Dub
Irish Bridge

seat

old shore-line

Gillerthwaite Bridge
old river bank

Wonadell Beck

"Gillerthwaite

104ft (32m)

High~
Cat Crag

Low~   Ennerdale Youth Hostel
Field Centre

The *Liza*, derived from *Lysa* (Norse), meaning bright water, drains the southern flanks of the *High Stile* range and the buttresses and coves of *Pillar, Great Gable and Steeple*, then flows down a long and very lonely valley.

The forestry road is a bridleway to BLACK SAIL YOUTH HOSTEL, a true mountain refuge for riders and ramblers en route for Wasdale or Buttermere over *Black Sail* or *Scarth Gap* plus fellwalkers and climbers bound for the crags and peaks of *Pillar, Gable or High Stile.*

Long 3° 19' W

Fellwalkers use these routes to gain access to *Haycock & Scoat Fell*

Heights above lake level of Ennerdale's Mountains :
High Stile 2274ft (693m), *Great Gable* 2580ft (786m), *Pillar* 2538ft (779m), *Steeple* 2318ft (706m), *Scoat Fell* 2391ft (729m), *Haycock* 2250ft (686m)

Long 3° 21' W   20' 30"   Long 3° 20' W   19' 30"

50

THE WESTERN LAKES
Some General Notes
plus
Supplementary Remarks to Lake Charts

SCATTERED villages serve this, perhaps England's remotest, shore and hinterland. Ice-scoured valleys fan out in a forthright manner to the plains from the Lake District's highest mountains. These constitute the toughest remnants of volcanic activity that took place over four hundred million years ago. Wast Water lies spectacularly in their midst. Indeed the view of the head of this lake serves as the very icon of the National Park. The other lakes in this group are based on the Skiddaw Slates - rocks even more ancient, almost as high but more rounded than the Borrowdale Volcanics. Granite extrudes on the western end of Wast Water and the head of Ennerdale Water. Red Pike, dominating the fields twixt Buttermere and Crummock Water, epitomises this rock in hue and mountain form .

South of the Sandstone buttresses of Saint Bee's Head ruler-straight tidelines define the Irish Sea. Only the Isle of Man breaks the horizon. Westerlies sweep salt air across the narrow plain. The Vikings arrived on these winds over a thousand years ago. During their establishment of the first permanent settlements in Ireland they had absorbed Christian worship and developed communities which they peaceably imported to the Cumbrian dales. Meanwhile their cousins were colonising America, Greenland, Russia, southern Italy and northern France. The French "Northmen" or Normans began an invasion at Hastings that somewhat overshadowed the parallel, domestic incursion over the Irish Sea, although it was generations behind, taking turn to subjugate the Dalesmen of the Lake District!

Wast Water and Ennerdale Water drain into the triple Ravenglass estuary while the remaining trio feed the Cocker, a tributary of the Derwent, that takes the waters from other lakes in the Northern Group. The tides of Ravenglass afford effortless canoeing for the very skilled, experienced and wary on the Esk, Mite and Irt. Lakeless Eskdale attracts visitors along the narrow-guage railway from Ravenglass. Muncaster Castle exudes history and houses the Owl Centre. The coal mines of the plain and their ports have a fascinating history too. Their closure caused great inter-war unemployment and deprivation, somewhat eclipsed by more publicised reports and demonstrations emanating from other industrial areas of Britain. The construction of Windscale Atomic Power Station hoped to redress the situation. More than just visitor attractions, these places are integral if legendary components of the area.

Copeland -"bought-land" (Norse)- District Council serves Wast Water and Ennerdale Water from Whitehaven, whereas Workington at the mouth of the Derwent administers Allerdale -"valley of the Ellen"- Council in which Lowes Water, Crummock Water and Buttermere lie. A huge detour to the north or south of the mountains is necessary for transport coming into the area. Although trains run along the coast between Barrow-in-Furness and Carlisle, access to the lakes by public transport is sparse. Ennerdale Bridge has a regular bus service, and a couple a day run to Buttermere village from Cockermouth. Otherwise one is restricted to minimal summer services. One such is the Egremont to Gosforth and Wasdale Youth Hostel, three-buses-a-day, on Saturdays and Bank Holidays during July and August only, route. The "Ennerdale Rambler", linking its namesake lake with other-sisters Lowes Water, Crummock Water and Buttermere, operates at weekends and Bank Holidays. Buttermere village is the connection for this, with a daily summer service, the "Honister Rambler", which serves the Whinlatter Pass and Honister Hause circuit from Keswick, passing Crummock Water and Buttermere twice in each direction.

Accommodation is likewise limited. Wast Water provides one example of every type of accommodation, but for Ennerdale Water the nearest overnights will be spent in B&Bs or farmhouses. Local villages have hotels and pubs. Lamplugh campsite between Ennerdale and Loweswater, open all year, takes caravans as well as tents. Youth Hostellers stay two miles up Ennerdale's forestry road beyond the lake or in Buttermere village (which also has a choice of tent-sites, traditional hotels and guest houses) and Cockermouth. Lowes Water has inns at either end supplemented by the Vale of Lorton's caravan sites. Crummock Water only offers private accommodation, but Buttermere village best serves as a base for activities centred on either of the twin lakes.

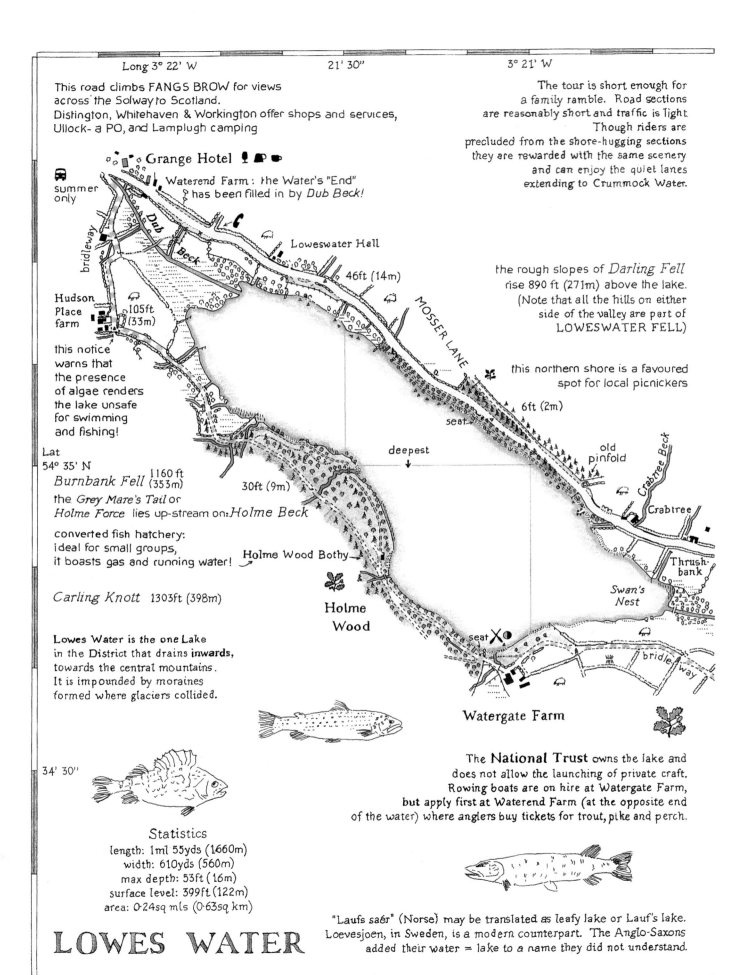

This road climbs FANGS BROW for views
across the Solway to Scotland.
Distington, Whitehaven & Workington offer shops and services,
Ullock- a PO, and Lamplugh camping

The tour is short enough for
a family ramble. Road sections
are reasonably short and traffic is light.
Though riders are
precluded from the shore-hugging sections
they are rewarded with the same scenery
and can enjoy the quiet lanes
extending to Crummock Water.

Grange Hotel

summer
only

Waterend Farm: the Water's "End"
? has been filled in by *Dub Beck*!

Loweswater Hall

bridleway

Dub Beck

46ft (14m)

MOSSER LANE

the rough slopes of *Darling Fell*
rise 890 ft (271m) above the lake.
(Note that all the hills on either
side of the valley are part of
LOWESWATER FELL)

Hudson
Place
farm

105ft
(33m)

this notice
warns that
the presence
of algae renders
the lake unsafe
for swimming
and fishing!

this northern shore is a favoured
spot for local picnickers

6ft (2m)

seat

old
pinfold

Crabtree Beck

Lat
54° 35' N

Burnbank Fell 1160 ft
(353m)

the *Grey Mare's Tail* or
Holme Force lies up-stream on *Holme Beck*

30ft (9m)

deepest
↓

Crabtree

converted fish hatchery:
ideal for small groups,
it boasts gas and running water!

Holme Wood Bothy

Thrush-
bank

Swan's
Nest

Carling Knott 1303ft (398m)

Holme
Wood

Lowes Water is the one Lake
in the District that drains **inwards**,
towards the central mountains.
It is impounded by moraines
formed where glaciers collided.

seat

bridleway

Watergate Farm

34' 30"

The **National Trust** owns the lake and
does not allow the launching of private craft.
Rowing boats are on hire at Watergate Farm,
but apply first at Waterend Farm (at the opposite end
of the water) where anglers buy tickets for trout, pike and perch.

Statistics
length: 1ml 55yds (1660m)
width: 610yds (560m)
max depth: 53ft (16m)
surface level: 399ft (122m)
area: 0·24sq mls (0·63sq km)

"Laufs saér" (Norse) may be translated as leafy lake or Lauf's lake.
Loevesjoen, in Sweden, is a modern counterpart. The Anglo-Saxons
added their water = lake to a name they did not understand.

LOWES WATER

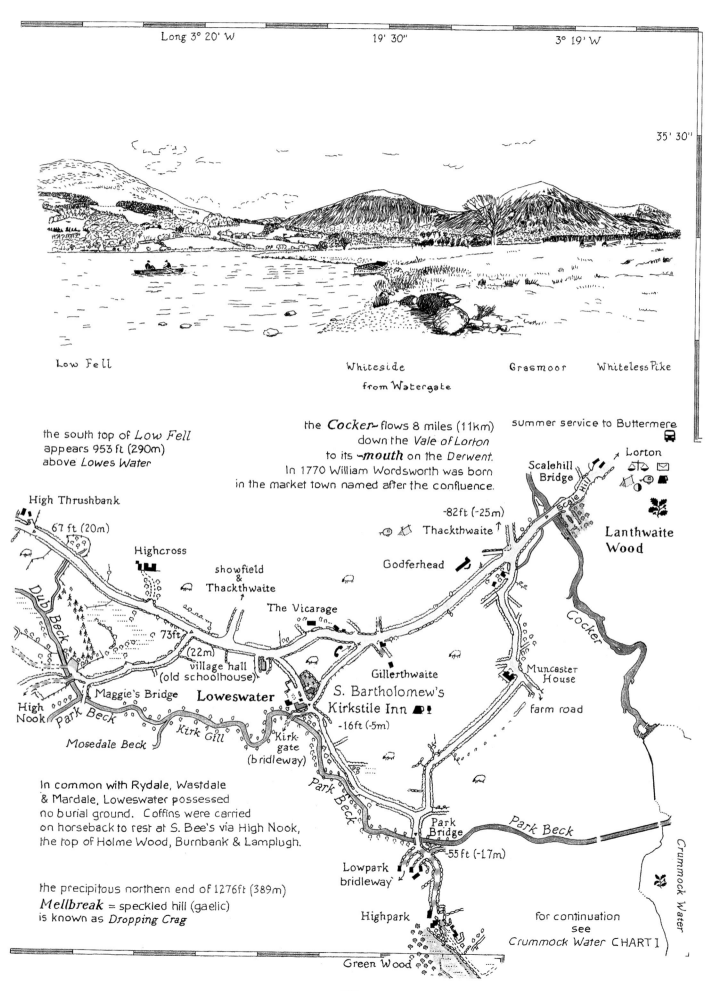

Low Fell

Whiteside

Grasmoor   Whiteless Pike

from Watergate

the south top of *Low Fell*
appears 953 ft (290m)
above *Lowes Water*

the *Cocker* flows 8 miles (11km)
down the *Vale of Lorton*
to its *mouth* on the *Derwent*.
In 1770 William Wordsworth was born
in the market town named after the confluence.

summer service to Buttermere

High Thrushbank

67 ft (20m)

Highcross

showfield
&
Thackthwaite

The Vicarage

-82ft (-25m)

Thackthwaite

Godferhead

Scalehill
Bridge

Lorton

Lanthwaite
Wood

Cocker

Dub Beck

73ft
(22m)
village hall
(old schoolhouse)

Maggie's Bridge   **Loweswater**

Gillerthwaite

**S. Bartholomew's
Kirkstile Inn**

-16ft (-5m)

Muncaster
House

farm road

High
Nook

Park Beck

Kirk Gill

Mosedale Beck

Kirk-
gate
(bridleway)

In common with Rydale, Wastdale
& Mardale, Loweswater possessed
no burial ground. Coffins were carried
on horseback to rest at S. Bee's via High Nook,
the top of Holme Wood, Burnbank & Lamplugh.

Park Beck

Park Beck

Park
Bridge

-55 ft (-17m)

the precipitous northern end of 1276ft (389m)
Mellbreak = speckled hill (gaelic)
is known as *Dropping Crag*

Lowpark
bridleway

Highpark

for continuation
see
Crummock Water CHART I

Crummock Water

Green Wood

53

WAST WATER: The Youth Hostel near the foot and the National Trust camp-site at the head of the lake have access to the water for portable boats. Due to its great depth and proximity to the open sea this lake reputedly never froze. When mains electricity was brought to Wasdale Head, underground cables preserved the visual amenity of the dale. Expense and effort were spared by submerging the cable in the lake. The shoreline serves as an outward or return "leg" of a fell-walking expedition over the summits of The Screes but is more arduous than the moorland section. Negotiating large or loose boulders and rocks or shifting scree results in tired and aching limbs for unseasoned scramblers.

ENNERDALE WATER is the only lake that can be walked round completely without treading tarmacadam or contending with motorised traffic on public roads. The southern shore has been adopted by the "Coast to Coast Walk". The chief recipients of the lake's water are the homes and businesses of Whitehaven.

LOWES WATER: A Romano-British settlement existed on the spur of Melbreak at Bargate to the south-east of the lake. Saint Bartholomew's Church dates from the 12th Century and was rebuilt in 1837. Saint Ninian baptised converts in his Well here. The focus of a scattered community, Kirkstile Inn once doubled as a farm. A hundred years ago a tragedy occurred when Crabtree Beck, swollen by the waters from a burst dam on Loweswater Fell, swept the bodies of an occupant and his child out of the eponymous house into the lake.

CRUMMOCK WATER: The level has been raised a few feet to supply the Cockermouth and Workington area. Melbreak, sometimes spelt Mellbreak, dominates Lowes Water and Crummock Water and provides a prime objective for walkers. The ascent blends conveniently with a round trip including a spell of damp shore-walking. Ranulph of Lindsaye, the benefactor of Saint Bee's Abbey, erected a pele tower on the moraine above the shore between Melbreak and the Cocker. It was defended from marauding Scots by a double moat. A succeeding farm, in turn defunct, was built from the remains. To the west isolated lead mines operated above streams draining to Park Beck. Cinderdale Beck on the east shore is named after ancient bloomeries - ancient hearths where iron was smelted from local ores. The ice ages produced a single lake which alluvium from Sail Beck and Sourmilk Gill divided into Crummock Water and....

BUTTERMERE: For the bus or car-bound, Honister and Newlands Hauses are exciting introductions to the deep trench cradling Buttermere and Crummock Water. Fleetwith Edge which threatens to tumble into the head of the lake was carved by adjoining glaciers. A mill operated above the church. Its millstream, Mill Beck, is channelled along the base of Long How directly into Crummock Water. No doubt Sail Beck, its feeder, left unharnessed, would continue to spread debris over the land it has created and flood the meadows we see today. The Fish Hotel was noted for its landlord's legendary daughter, the beautiful Mary of Buttermere. Her tale is recounted in several books. Hassness and the Youth Hostel are former hotels. Inside Saint James' Church a memorial induces appreciative fellwalkers to pay homage to A. Wainwright, creator of the famous Fell Guides. His ashes are scattered atop his favourite Haystacks. This hill's precipitous, brooding flanks dominate Warnscale Bottom at the head of the lake.

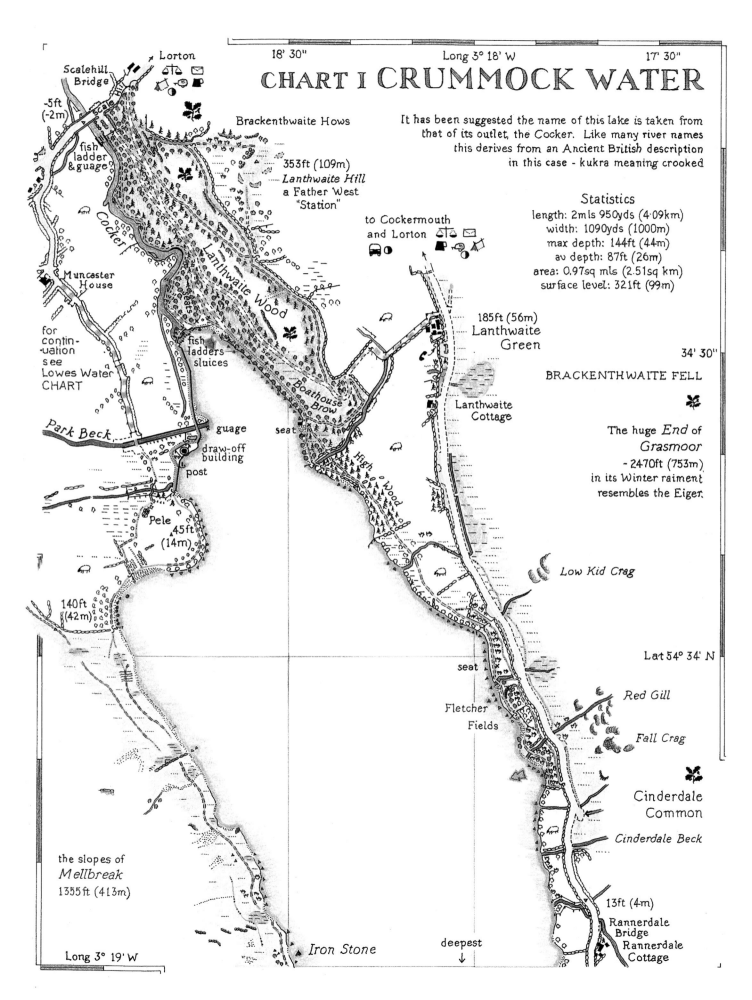

CHART I CRUMMOCK WATER

Scalehill Bridge

Lorton

-5ft (-2m)

scale

fish ladder & guage

Brackenthwaite Hows

353ft (109m)
Lanthwaite Hill
a Father West
"Station"

to Cockermouth
and Lorton

It has been suggested the name of this lake is taken from
that of its outlet, the Cocker. Like many river names
this derives from an Ancient British description
in this case - kukra meaning crooked

Statistics
length: 2mls 950yds (4·09km)
width: 1090yds (1000m)
max depth: 144ft (44m)
av depth: 87ft (26m)
area: 0.97sq mls (2.51sq km)
surface level: 321ft (99m)

Cocker

Muncaster House

Lanthwaite Wood

seats

for contin-
-uation
see
Lowes Water
CHART

fish
ladders
sluices

Boathouse Brow

Park Beck

guage

draw-off
building

post

seat

185ft (56m)
Lanthwaite
Green

34' 30"

BRACKENTHWAITE FELL

Lanthwaite
Cottage

The huge *End* of
Grasmoor
- 2470ft (753m)
in its Winter raiment
resembles the Eiger.

Pele

45ft (14m)

High Wood

140ft (42m)

Low Kid Crag

Lat 54° 34' N

the slopes of
Mellbreak
1355ft (413m)

seat

Fletcher
Fields

Red Gill

Fall Crag

Cinderdale
Common

Cinderdale Beck

13ft (4m)
Rannerdale
Bridge
Rannerdale
Cottage

Iron Stone

deepest
↓

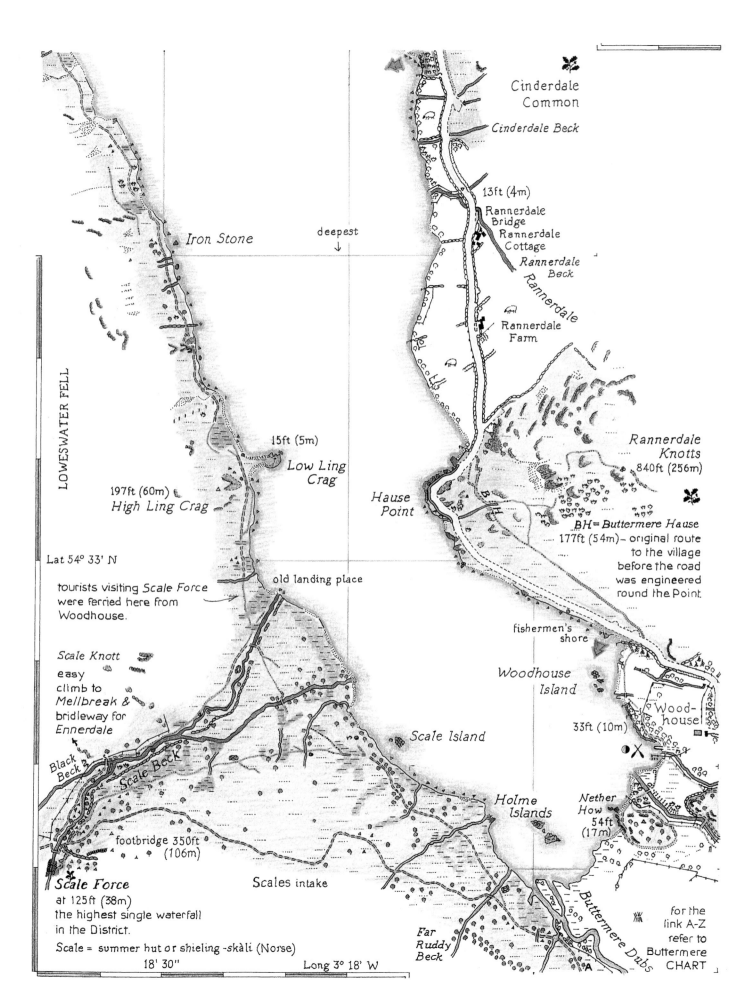

Cinderdale
Common

Cinderdale Beck

13ft (4m)

Rannerdale
Bridge
Rannerdale
Cottage

*Rannerdale
Beck*

Rannerdale

Rannerdale
Farm

*Rannerdale
Knotts*
840ft (256m)

BH = Buttermere Hause
177ft (54m) - original route
to the village
before the road
was engineered
round the Point

Iron Stone

deepest
↓

15ft (5m)

*Low Ling
Crag*

197ft (60m)
High Ling Crag

LOWESWATER FELL

Lat 54° 33' N

tourists visiting *Scale Force*
were ferried here from
Woodhouse.

Scale Knott
easy
climb to
Mellbreak &
bridleway for
Ennerdale

*Black
Beck*

Scale Beck

footbridge 350ft
(106m)

Scales intake

Scale Force
at 125ft (38m)
the highest single waterfall
in the District.

Scale = summer hut or shieling -skàli (Norse)

18' 30"

*Hause
Point*

old landing place

Scale Island

*Holme
Islands*

*Far
Ruddy
Beck*

fishermen's
shore

*Woodhouse
Island*

33ft (10m)

Wood-
house

*Nether
How*
54ft
(17m)

Buttermere Dubs

for the
link A-Z
refer to
Buttermere
CHART

Long 3° 18' W

56

✤ CHART II CRUMMOCK WATER

Decide whether
Rannerdale
is derived from: Ravens' Dale
from hravner-dalr (Norse) or
Ragnar whose descendant, Buthar
successfully resisted Norman armed
dominance. Nicholas Size's novel,
The Secret Valley dramatises this
episode in the history of the valley.

Bowness Knott from north-west shore

The permitted path to Nether How below Woodhouse is brand new.
To continue the circuit of Crummock Water a detour, necessarily avoiding
sensitive marsh and farmland, has to be made. Follow Mill Beck
to the car park at Buttermere village, then the farm road onto
Scale Bridge which appears on the Buttermere CHART, q.v.

The NT impose a limit of 10 craft
for CANOEING, DINGHY SAILING
& ROWING and control the FISHING
for the trout, salmon, char, pike and perch.
There are no facilities for launching, so boats
will require man-handling from vehicles or trailers
and powered craft are not allowed on the water.
Apply for PERMITS for any of these activities at
Woodhouse, where ROWING BOATS may be HIRED.

Wilderness
Wood

Hagg Sike

112ft (34m)

155ft (47m)

Long How

Crag Houses

Longhow
Wood

Sail Beck

Keswick
via Newlands Hause
776ft (237m)

Mill Beck

George VI
Memorial
Youth Hostel

B

WC

F C

S

Z

▲ = 55ft (17m)

157ft
(48m)

BUTTERMERE

KEY TO FACILITIES·

B = BRIDGE HOTEL   C = CROFT HOUSE FARM
F = FISH HOTEL   H = PARISH HALL (OLD SCHOOL)
J = PARISH CHURCH OF S JAMES THE GREAT
S = SYKE FARM (FOR   -ACROSS MILL BECK)

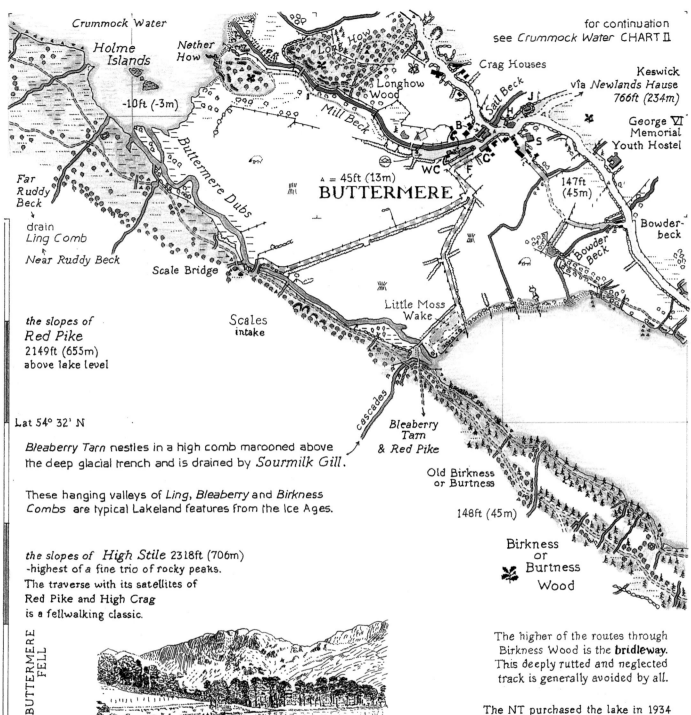

Crummock Water

Holme Islands

-10ft (-3m)

Nether How

Long How

for continuation
see *Crummock Water* CHART II

Crag Houses

Longhow Wood

Mill Beck

Sail Beck

J

B

H

C

F

C

F

L

S

WC

Keswick
via *Newlands Hause*
766ft (234m)

George VI
Memorial
Youth Hostel

△ = 45ft (13m)

BUTTERMERE

147ft
(45m)

Bowder-
beck

Bowder
Beck

Far
Ruddy
Beck

drain
Ling Comb

Near Ruddy Beck

Buttermere Dubs

Scale Bridge

Scales
intake

Little Moss
Wake

the slopes of
Red Pike
2149ft (655m)
above lake level

Lat 54° 32' N

Bleaberry Tarn nestles in a high comb marooned above
the deep glacial trench and is drained by *Sourmilk Gill*.

These hanging valleys of *Ling, Bleaberry* and *Birkness*
Combs are typical Lakeland features from the Ice Ages.

cascades

Bleaberry
Tarn
& Red Pike

Old Birkness
or Burtness

148ft (45m)

the slopes of *High Stile* 2318ft (706m)
-highest of a fine trio of rocky peaks.
The traverse with its satellites of
Red Pike and High Crag
is a fellwalking classic.

BUTTERMERE FELL

31' 30"

Birkness
or
Burtness
Wood

The higher of the routes through
Birkness Wood is the **bridleway**.
This deeply rutted and neglected
track is generally avoided by all.

The NT purchased the lake in 1934
and issue FISHING and BOATING PERMITS
(moderate daily fees) available from Dalegarth
where ROWING BOATS may be hired by the hour.
Char, pike and perch inhabit the waters but
trout are the main lure for the angling fraternity.
A limit of 10 craft at any one time is imposed
for canoeing, windsurfing, dinghy sailing & rowing.
Of course powered craft are not allowed on the lake.

Haystacks

Statistics
length: 1mile 465yds (2.03km)
width: 650yds (600m)
area: 0.36sq mls (0.93 sq km)
depth: 94ft (28m)
av depth: 54ft (16m)
surface level: 331ft (101m)

To distinguish lake from village
a qualifying noun can only be appended to the
latter as the present settlement was named after the "mere".
The name may be derived from either buðar=huts (Norse) or
butere=dairy pastures (Old English) + mere=lake (Old Eng).

BUTTERMERE

17' 30"   Long 3° 17' W   16' 30"   Long 3°

KEY TO FACILITIES

B = BRIDGE HOTEL 🍺 C = CROFT HOUSE FARM 🍴
F = FISH HOTEL 🍺 H = PARISH HALL (OLD SCHOOL)
J = PARISH CHURCH OF S. JAMES THE GREAT
S = SYKE FARM (FOR 🍴 -ACROSS MILL BECK)

Snock Rigg 🌿

from Green Crag

Long Crag

Pike Rigg

108ft (33m)

Birkness

Dale-garth

the tunnel

Hassness

Hassnesshow Beck
drains *Goat Gills*

Kirk Close

Muddock Crags

Lambing Knott

mine

10ft (3m)

Lower Gatescarth

Birk or Burt Ness
seat

deepest
↓

Horse Close

seat

Comb Beck
drains
Birkness
or *Burtness*
Comb

Low Crag

Char Cottage

56ft (17m)

Hartley Beck

Gatescarthdale Beck

Gatescarth

the slopes of
High Crag
2113ft (643m)

Peggy's Bridge

SG

Warnscale Beck

Borrowdale & Derwent Water
via the notorious *Honister Hause*,
a very steep climb of 846ft (255m)

Warnscale Bottom

bridleway over *Scarth Gap*, 1130ft (344m), to *Ennerdale*

Lat 54° 32' N

Few mountains in Britain are named
after people. Here is
a Cumbrian example
– *Robinson*
2087 ft (636m)
above the lake

BUTTERMERE FELL

31' 30"

16' W   15' 30"   Long 3° 15' W   14' 30"

THE NORTHERN LAKES
Some General Notes
plus
Supplementary Remarks to Lake Charts

THIS GROUP is divided between three lakes associated with the Derwent and three within the watershed of Cumbria's major river, the Eden, which empties into the Solway Firth. The area provides the greatest variety of lake scenery. The heads of Bassenthwaite Lake and Haweswater Reservoir are classic territory for wildfowl and birds of prey respectively. Bassenthwaite lies on Skiddaw Slate; Thirlmere, like Haweswater, on volcanic rocks. Being situated at a greater altitude these latter were prized by the water engineers who required as great a height differentiation as possible to siphon Lakeland's pure waters into Manchester's factories and homes. Ullswater's three reaches illustrate a scenic progression from precipitous crag to farmland. In common with Derwent Water it lies on a division between these rock types. The spectacular line of crags along the eastern shore of the latter are volcanic rocks, standing above Skiddaw Slates, eroded by glaciers.

Apart from Haweswater Reservoir, these lakes have been extremely accessible since the construction of a trunk road to the West Coast ports from the motorway south of Penrith. Instead of creating a more direct link with the county seat and regional centres at Carlisle and Newcastle across the Solway Plain and through the Tyne Gap, the greatest act of corporate vandalism yet perpetrated on the National Park was undertaken in the 1960s and 70s. The character of a huge slice of the landscape is altered - a sad exchange for the railway which served this very route and whose destruction coincided with the development of the arterial road. Keswick is the focus for bus services in the northern half of the Lake District. The Stagecoach Express connects along the afore-mentioned trunk route to Cockermouth alternating along either shore of Bassenthwaite Lake (useful for canoeists running the Derwent into the Lake). Another, the "Lakes Link", runs north, on the east shore only, to Wigton and Carlisle or south past Thirlmere Reservoir to Ambleside. The "Borrowdale Rambler" provides a regular service along the east shore of Derwent Water. The "Honister Rambler" is a summer-only bus ride doing twice-daily circuits in each direction along the west shore to Grange-in-Borrowdale, over Honister Hause to Buttermere, with a return over Whinlatter Pass. Penrith is served by the West Coast railway. Ullswater sees the comings and goings of the Patterdale Bus along the main road from this market town. Brothers Water lies short of this service, which is only extended in the Summer by the "Kirkstone Rambler" which links the two largest lakes in the Lake District thrice a day. Between May and the school holidays this runs on weekends and Bank Holidays only. The Post-Bus serves the south side of Ullswater on weekday morning and afternoon out-and-home runs (morning-only on Saturdays) from Penrith. Finally, "Haweswater Ramblers" set out every Saturday, Sunday and Bank Holiday during May to Late September from Penrith Bus Station via Askham and Bampton for Mardale Head.

Keswick is the last word in accommodation. Derwent Water and Ullswater are surrounded by hotels, hostels, guest houses and campsites, nearly all commanding tremendous prospects. Bassenthwaite, Thirlmere Reservoir and Brothers Water have traditional hotels and established campsites nearby. Haweswater Reservoir has its custom-built hotel which serves daytime and overnight visitors in its splendid isolation. The closest camp-sites lie above Ullswater. Inns and B&Bs exist in the villages to the east in an extensive area bereft of Youth Hostels, but containing a single camping and caravanning site - Lowther Holiday Park.

The Eden Valley and Back o' Skidda' is riddled with often imposing, nationally important monuments dating from prehistory, through the Dark Ages to the present times. Peaceful off-days, indeed a whole holiday, may be interestingly spent viewing stone circles, Roman remains, abbeys, mediæval castles, stately homes and old villages that are architectural and visual delights.

This group of lakes is shared between Allerdale and Eden District Councils based at Workington and Penrith respectively. The National Park Authority issues *Lake User's Guides* to Bassenthwaite Lake, Derwent Water and Ullswater which up-date access and facilities.

A long-distance footpath, the "Allerdale Ramble", follows the west shore of Derwent Water and the link with Bassenthwaite Lake which it passes on the eastern side, *en route* for Cockermouth.

BASSENTHWAITE LAKE is flanked by the trunk road that severs the northern part of the Lake District. Nevertheless it constitutes the most important inland refuge for bird life thanks to the extensive wetland area at the head of the lake. Accordingly the authorities have created a National Nature Reserve and restrict boating activities. Before taking to the water do ensure you have acquired a relevant permit from a National Park Centre or other outlet. The Knott Head lay-by on Whinlatter Pass, some 450 feet (135 metres) above the Lake, gives a wonderful view of Skiddaw rearing above its marshy headwaters.

DERWENT WATER vies with Windermere in popularity thanks to its proximity to Keswick, the hub of the district, and its varied and grander scenery. It possesses more habitable islands and is very shallow considering its extent - it is the widest. This lake and its valley, Borrowdale, have always attracted artists, scientists, geologists, poets and pioneering conservationists. Most of the shoreline is public, and the launches serve seven strategically positioned stages all year round. During December till mid-March only a weekend timetable operates, though groups may arrange weekday sailings during these winter periods; indeed special cruises and excursions are available throughout the year. Saint Kentigern or Mungo, Bishop of Glasgow, suffered banishment by the King of Strathclyde and Cumbria. En route to Saint David in Wales, he began the conversion of the Cumbrian people, erecting a great cross in a clearing at a spot that became known as Crosthwaite. "Thwaite" (Norse) means clearing or field. In the 12th Century the Lady of Allerdale had the first of five churches built on this site between the two lakes. The latest restoration of the great Parish Church of the Vale of Keswick took place in 1844.

Plumbago and lead mines expanded in the 17th and 18th Centuries and account for Keswick's pencil industry. Ore and coal from the plain were ferried across the lake avoiding near-impassable marsh to its north. Hest Holm (horse island) is the earliest of several names for Derwent Isle. This was gardened by German miners introduced in Queen Elizabeth I's time to work the royal copper mines west of the lake. William Wordsworth did not approve of the mock antiquities, Georgian mansion and belfried boat house built on Derwent Isle after its purchase in 1778 by Joseph Pocklington of Nottingham. This eccentric arranged regattas and mock battles, appointing Peter Crosthwaite, a retired naval commander, as Admiral of his "Fleet". The latter gentleman surveyed elegant and accurate maps of the Lakes and sold them from the museum he founded at The Quadrant, Telescope and Weathercock in Keswick.

14th Century Finkle Street led pilgrims to Nichol End Landing where they embarked for Saint Herbert's Isle. This recluse's primitive hut of wood and turf would soon rot and disappear. The remains seen today are the work of more modern hands. Beatrix Potter readers, young and not so young, will recognise this as Owl Island to which the Squirrels Nutkin, Twinkleberry and cousins voyaged for nuts using their tails as sails. Benjamin Bunny's exploits took place in Fawe Park's garden.

The Radcliffe family came from the north-east of England where they lost land during the Civil War. The dynasty's occupation of Lord's Island ended when the Earl of Derwentwater lost his head after rising in support of the Old Pretender. The sculpted split boulder on the north shore of Calfclose Bay commemorates all who helped the National Trust to acquire Lakeland properties during the first century of its existence, 1895-1995. It is the work of Peter Randell-Page.

Apart from Canon Hardwicke (1851-1920), the radical triumvirate of National Trust founders included Octavia Hill and Sir Robert Hunter. Octavia Hill, with the financial help of John Ruskin, devoted herself to the welfare of poor families. Sir Robert Hunter was a lawyer who fought for the preservation of open spaces and was associated with the Commons Protection Society. The first Lake District acquisition was Brandlehow Park, purchased by public subscription. Manesty Park was added five years later.

Imposing spoil heaps at High Brandlehow are evidence of the important lead mining activities which began before the Romans came. A steam engine and huge water-wheel eventually failed to keep pace with flooding in the extensive shafts. Above rock-girt Brandlehow Point, Sir Hugh Walpole made his home at Brackenburn. A highly successful historical novelist whose famous "Herries Chronicles" series are set in old-time Borrowdale, he died during the Second World War.

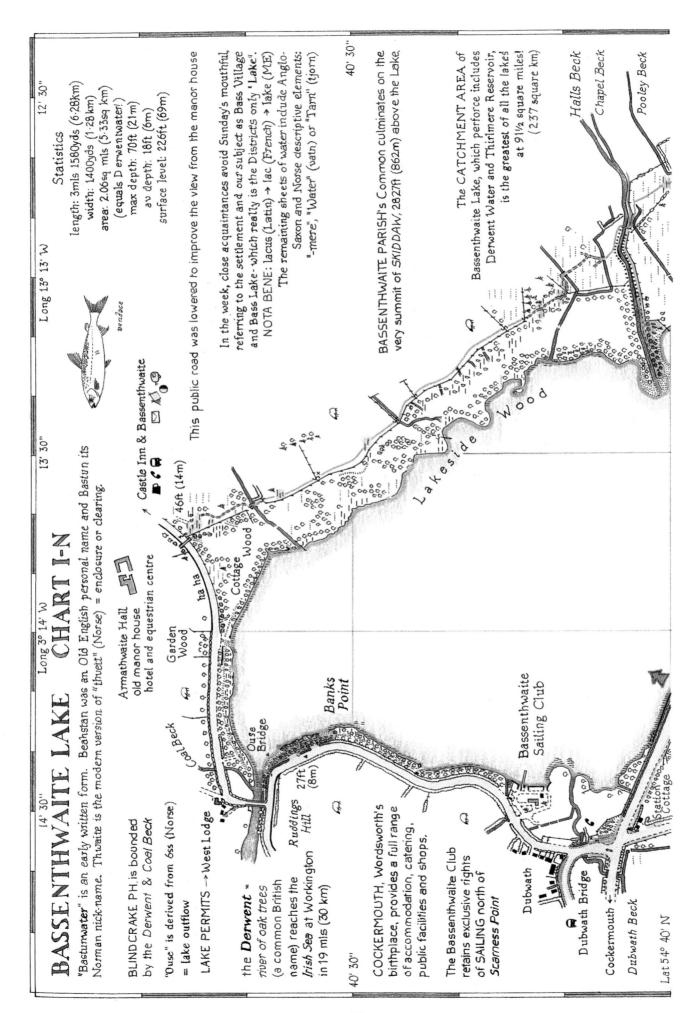

BASSENTHWAITE LAKE   CHART I-N

Statistics

length: 3mls 1580yds (6·28km)
width: 1400yds (1·28km)
area: 2·06sq mls (5·33sq km)
(equals Derwentwater!)
max depth: 70ft (21m)
av depth: 18ft (6m)
surface level: 226ft (69m)

14' 30"   13' 30"   Long 13° 13' W   12' 30"

40' 30"

"*Basturwater*" is an early written form. Beohstan was an Old English personal name and Bas un its Norman nick-name. Thwaite is the modern version of "thveit" (Norse) = enclosure or clearing.

BLINDCRAKE PH. is bounded by the *Derwent* & *Coal Beck*

"*Ouse*" is derived from óss (Norse) = lake outflow

LAKE PERMITS → West Lodge

the **Derwent** = river of oak trees (a common British name) reaches the *Irish Sea* at *Workington* in 19 mls (30 km)

COCKERMOUTH, Wordsworth's birthplace, provides a full range of accommodation, catering, public facilities and shops.

The Bassenthwaite Club retains exclusive rights of SAILING north of *Scarness Point*

vendace

Armathwaite Hall old manor house hotel and equestrian centre

↑ Castle Inn & Bassenthwaite

This public road was lowered to improve the view from the manor house

In the week, close acquaintances avoid Sunday's mouthful, referring to the settlement and our subject as Bass Village and Bass Lake - which really is the Districts only "Lake". NOTA BENE: lacus (Latin) → lac (French) → lake (ME) The remaining sheets of water include Anglo-Saxon and Norse descriptive elements: "-mere", "Water" (vatn) or "Tarn" (tjörn)

BASSENTHWAITE PARISH's Common culminates on the very summit of *SKIDDAW*, 2827ft (862m) above the Lake.

The CATCHMENT AREA of Bassenthwaite Lake, which perforce includes Derwent Water and Thirlmere Reservoir, is the greatest of all the lakes at 91½ square miles! (237 square km)

Halls Beck
Chapel Beck
Pooley Beck

Coal Beck
46ft (14m)
Cottage Wood
Garden Wood
ha ha
Ouse Bridge
Ruddings Hill
27ft (8m)
Banks Point

Lakeside Wood

Bassenthwaite Sailing Club

Station Cottage

Dubwath
Dubwath Bridge
Cockermouth →
Dubwath Beck

40' 30"

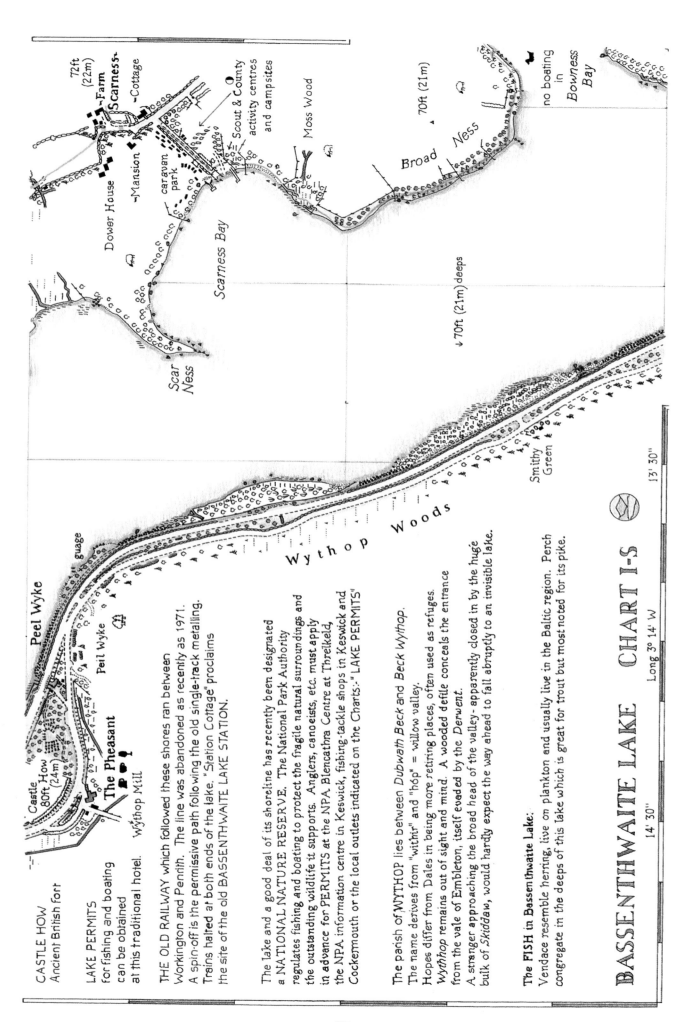

BASSENTHWAITE LAKE   CHART 1-S

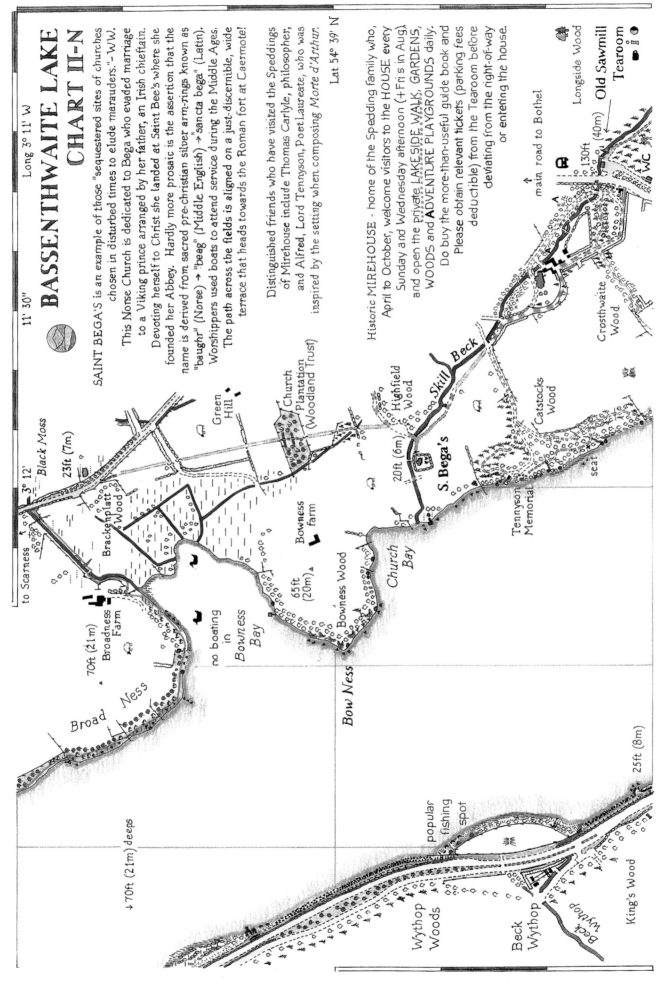

BASSENTHWAITE LAKE
CHART II-N

Long 3° 11' W

11' 30"

Lat 54° 39' N

SAINT BEGA'S is an example of those "sequestered sites of churches chosen in disturbed times to elude marauders."- W.W.

This Norse Church is dedicated to Bega who evaded marriage to a Viking prince arranged by her father, an Irish chieftain. Devoting herself to Christ she landed at Saint Bee's where she founded her Abbey. Hardly more prosaic is the assertion that the name is derived from sacred pre-christian silver arm-rings known as "baughr" (Norse) → "beag" (Middle English) → "sancta bega" (Latin). Worshippers used boats to attend service during the Middle Ages. The path across the fields is aligned on a just-discernible, wide terrace that heads towards the Roman fort at Caermote!

Distinguished friends who have visited the Speddings of Mirehouse include Thomas Carlyle, philosopher, and Alfred, Lord Tennyson, Poet Laureate, who was inspired by the setting when composing *Morte d'Arthur.*

Historic **MIREHOUSE** - home of the Spedding family who, April to October, welcome visitors to the HOUSE every Sunday and Wednesday afternoon (+Fri's in Aug), and open the private LAKESIDE WALK, GARDENS, WOODS and **ADVENTURE PLAYGROUNDS** daily. Do buy the more-than-useful guide book and Please obtain relevant tickets (parking fees deductible) from the Tearoom before deviating from the right-of-way or entering the house.

Longside Wood

Old Sawmill Tearoom

main road to Bothel

130ft

WC

(40m)

Crosthwaite Wood.

Skill Beck

Highfield Wood

20ft (6m)

S. Bega's

Catstocks Wood

Church Bay

Tennyson Memorial

seat

Bow Ness

65ft (20m)

Bowness Wood

Bowness farm

no boating in *Bowness Bay*

Green Hill

Church Plantation (Woodland Trust)

Black Moss

23ft (7m)

3° 12'

to Scarness

Brackenplatt Wood

70ft (21m) Broadness Farm

Broad Ness

↓70ft (21m) deeps

Wythop Woods

popular fishing spot

25ft (8m)

Beck Wythop

King's Wood

64

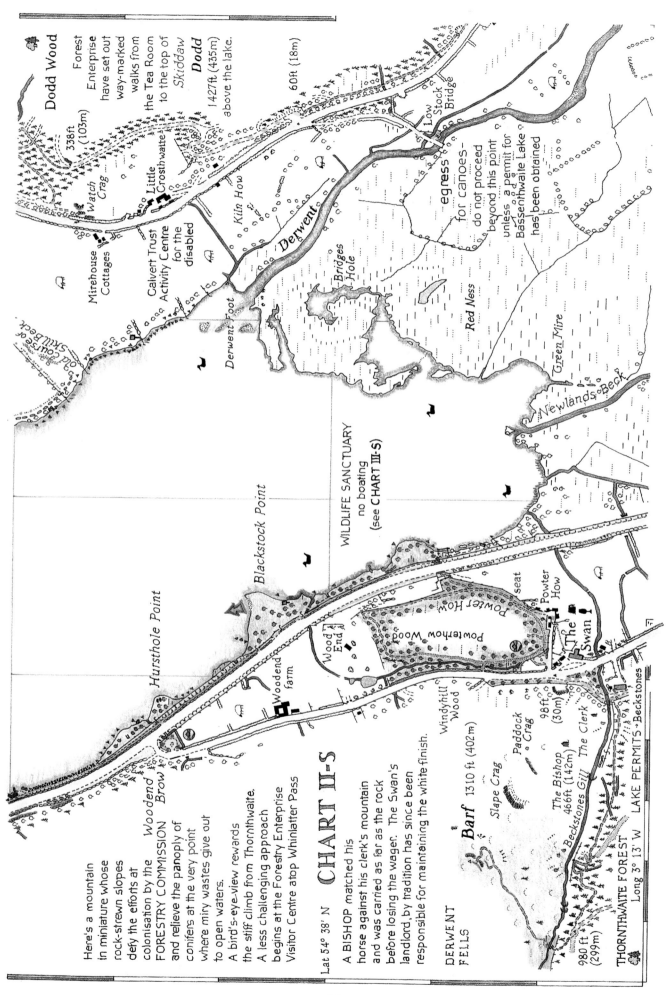

Dodd Wood

Forest Enterprise have set out way-marked walks from the Tea Room to the top of *Skiddaw*

Dodd 1427ft (435m)

338ft (103m)

60ft (18m) above the lake.

Watch Crag

Little Crosthwaite

Kiln How

Calvert Trust Activity Centre for the disabled

Mirehouse Cottages

Old course of Skill Beck

Derwent

Derwent Foot

Low Stock Bridge

egress for canoes – do not proceed beyond this point unless a permit for Bassenthwaite Lake has been obtained

Bridges Hole

Red Ness

Green Mire

Newlands Beck

WILDLIFE SANCTUARY no boating (see CHART III-S)

Blackstock Point

Hursthole Point

FORESTRY COMMISSION

Woodend Brow

Woodend farm

Wood End

Powterhow Wood

Powter How

seat

Powter How

The Swan

Windyhill Wood

98ft (30m)

Paddock Crag

Slape Crag

The Bishop 466ft (142m)

Beckstones Gill The Clerk

→ Beckstones

LAKE PERMITS

THORNTHWAITE FOREST

980 ft (299m)

DERWENT FELLS

Barf 1310 ft (402m)

Lat 54° 38′ N   **CHART II-S**   Long 3° 13′ W

Here's a mountain in miniature whose rock-strewn slopes defy the efforts at colonisation by the FORESTRY COMMISSION and relieve the panoply of conifers at the very point where miry wastes give out to open waters.
A bird's-eye-view rewards the stiff climb from Thornthwaite.
A less challenging approach begins at the Forestry Enterprise Visitor Centre atop Whinlatter Pass

A BISHOP matched his horse against his clerk's mountain and was carried as far as the rock before losing the wager. The Swan's landlord, by tradition has since been responsible for maintaining the white finish.

65

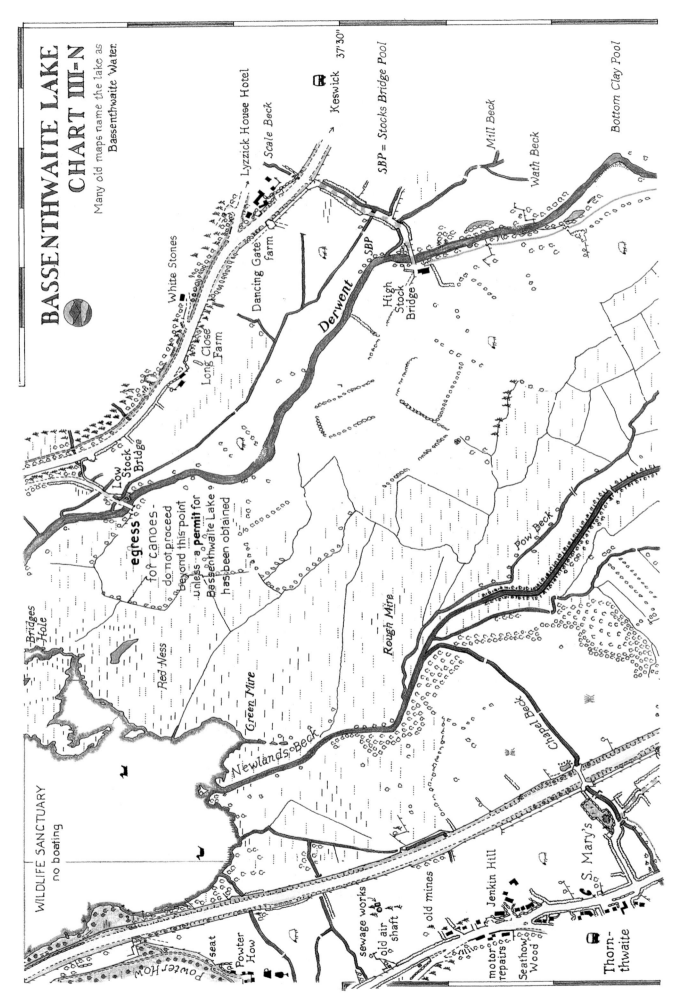

BASSENTHWAITE LAKE
CHART III-N

Many old maps name the lake as
Bassenthwaite Water.

White Stones

Long Close
Farm

Lyzzick House Hotel

Scale Beck

Keswick 37'30"

→ Keswick

Dancing Gate
farm

SBP = Stocks Bridge Pool

Mill Beck

Wath Beck

Bottom Clay Pool

Derwent

SBP

High
Stock
Bridge

Low
Stock
Bridge

egress
for canoes -
do not proceed
beyond this point
unless a **permit** for
Bassenthwaite Lake
has been obtained

Bridges
Hole

Red Ness

Green Mire

Rough Mire

Pow Beck

Newlands Beck

Chapel Beck

WILDLIFE SANCTUARY
no boating

Powter How

seat

Powter
How

sewage works

old air
shaft

old mines

Jenkin Hill

S. Mary's

motor
repairs

Seathow
Wood

Thorn-
thwaite

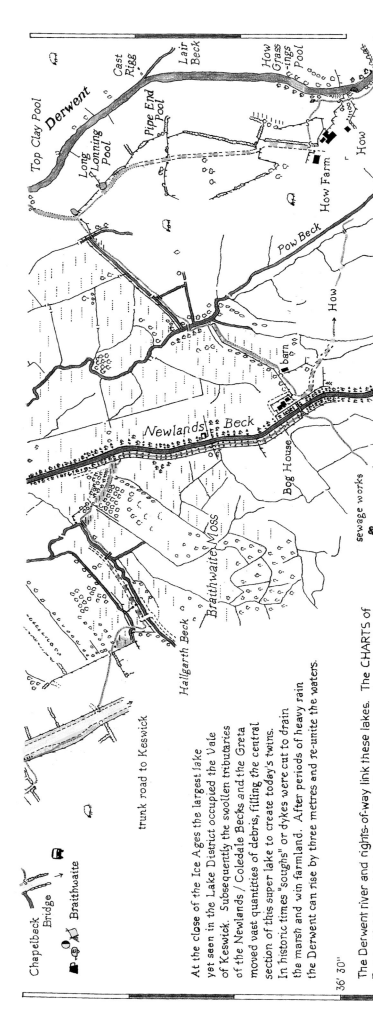

Top Clay Pool

Derwent

Cast Rigg

Lair Beck

Long Lonning Pool

Pipe End Pool

How Grass-ings Pool

How Farm

How

abandoned railway

Dick Tyson Island

Pow Beck

How

barn

Newlands Beck

Bog House

sewage works

Braithwaite

Braithwaite Moss

Hallgarth Beck

trunk road to Keswick

Chapelbeck Bridge

Braithwaite

trunk road

Portinscale

Braithwaite

Cockermouth

At the close of the Ice Ages the largest lake yet seen in the Lake District occupied the Vale of Keswick. Subsequently the swollen tributaries of the Newlands / Coledale Becks and the Greta moved vast quantities of debris, filling the central section of this super lake to create today's twins. In historic times "soughs" or dykes were cut to drain the marsh and win farmland. After periods of heavy rain the Derwent can rise by three metres and re-unite the waters.

The Derwent river and rights-of-way link these lakes. The CHARTS of Derwent Water and Bassenthwaite Lake are integrated to the same end.

The paddle from Derwent Water to Bassenthwaite Lake is a mild river-run for the experienced. CANOEISTS descending the Derwent from Keswick are subject to reasonable SEASONAL RESTRICTIONS - brokered by the British Canoe Union and Keswick Angling Association. (See across)

The EGRESS point at Low Stock Bridge might spare river-running, kayaker types the effort of paddling across flat water. Otherwise a National Park PERMIT to enter BASSENTHWAITE LAKE must have been obtained.

The head of Bassenthwaite Lake, south of Blackstock Point is a WILDLIFE SANCTUARY from which boat-users launching from the shores are excluded. Canoeists emerging from the Derwent are required to keep moving along the eastern shoreline and onto open water, making the least disturbance.

CANOES are PERMITTED on the RIVER:
NOVEMBER to MARCH
(Please be aware salmon spawn in the shallows during December, January & February. Disturbance of these areas, technically a criminal as well as an ecological offence, will occur when water levels are low.)
APRIL to JUNE
(But vacate the river before 4 P.M.)

Canoes are FORBIDDEN:
December to February - when levels are low.
April to June - after 4 P.M.
JULY to OCTOBER - at any time, under any conditions.

for - continuation see *Derwent Water* CHART I-N

BASSENTHWAITE LAKE   CHART III-S

Long 3° 12' W   11' 30"   10' 30"   Long 3° 11' W

36' 30"

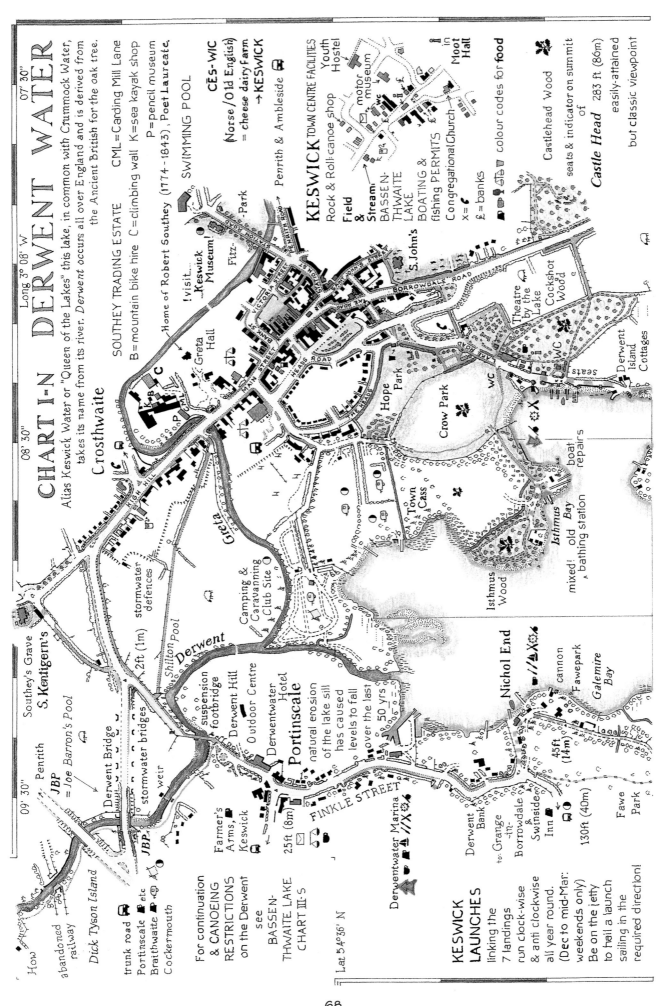

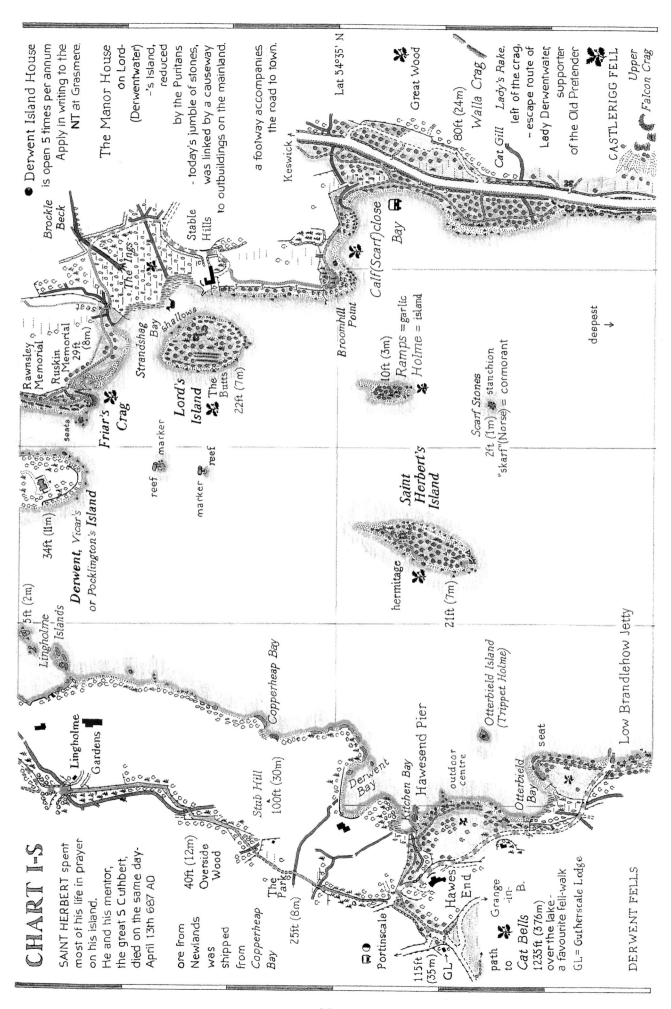

CHART I-S

SAINT HERBERT spent most of his life in prayer on his island.

He and his mentor, the great S Cuthbert, died on the same day - April 13th 687 AD

ore from Newlands was shipped from Copperheap Bay

Copperheap Bay

The Parks

Stub Hill 100ft (30m)

25ft (8m)

40ft (12m) Overside Wood

Lingholme Islands

5ft (2m)

Lingholme Gardens

34ft (11m)

Derwent, Vicar's or Pocklington's Island

reef marker

marker reef

Friar's Crag

Rawnsley Memorial

Ruskin Memorial 29ft (8m)

seat

seats

Strandshag Bay

Shallows

Lord's Island

The Butts 22ft (7m)

Brockle Beck

The Ings

Stable Hills

Keswick

Lat 54°35' N

Great Wood

80ft (24m)

Walla Crag

Cat Gill Lady's Rake, left of the crag, - escape route of Lady Derwentwater supporter of the Old Pretender

CASTLERIGG FELL

Upper Falcon Crag

Broomhill Point

Calf (Scarf) close Bay

Ramps = garlic
Holme = island

10ft (3m)

Scarf Stones

2ft (1m) stanchion
"skarf" (Norse) = cormorant

deepest →

Saint Herbert's Island

hermitage

21ft (7m)

Copperheap Bay

Derwent Bay

Kitchen Bay

Hawesend Pier

outdoor centre

Otterbield Island (Trippet Holme)

seat

Otterbield Bay

Low Brandlehow Jetty

Portinscale

115ft (35m)

GL→

path to Cat Bells 1235ft (376m) over the lake - a favourite fell-walk

GL = Gutherscale Ledge

Hawes End

Grange -in- B.

DERWENT FELLS

- Derwent Island House is open 5 times per annum Apply in writing to the NT at Grasmere.

The Manor House on Lord- (Derwentwater) -'s Island, reduced by the Puritans - today's jumble of stones, was linked by a causeway to outbuildings on the mainland.

a footway accompanies the road to town.

69

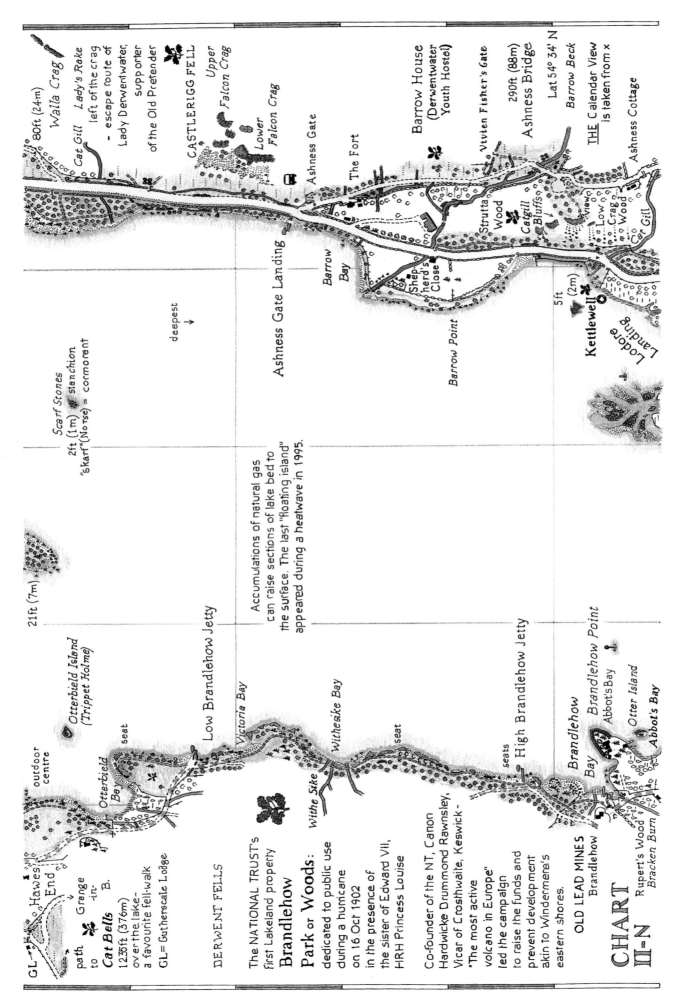

80ft (24m) *Walla Crag*

Cat Gill *Lady's Rake* left of the crag – escape route of Lady Derwentwater, supporter of the Old Pretender

CASTLERIGG FELL

Upper *Falcon Crag*

Lower *Falcon Crag*

Ashness Gate

The Fort

Barrow House (Derwentwater Youth Hostel)

Vivien Fisher's Gate

290ft (88m) Ashness Bridge

Lat 54° 34' N

Barrow Beck

THE Calendar View is taken from x

Ashness Cottage

Ashness Gate Landing

Barrow Bay

Strutta Wood

Catgill Bluffs

Shep- herd's Close

Barrow Point

5ft (2m)

Low Crag Wood

Cat Gill

Kettlewell

Lodore Landing

deepest →

Scarf Stones
2ft (1m) ≋ stanchion
"skarf"(Norse) = cormorant

Accumulations of natural gas can raise sections of lake bed to the surface. The last "floating island" appeared during a heatwave in 1995.

21ft (7m)

Otterbield Island (Trippet Holme)

Low Brandlehow Jetty

Victoria Bay

Withesike Bay

High Brandlehow Jetty

Brandlehow Bay

Brandlehow Point

Abbot's Bay

Otter Island

Abbot's Bay

seat

seat

seat

seats

outdoor centre

Otterbield Bay

GL—→ Hawes End
path to Grange -in- B.
Cat Bells
1235ft (376m) over the lake – a favourite fell-walk
GL= Gutherscale Lodge

DERWENT FELLS

The NATIONAL TRUST's first Lakeland property
Brandlehow Park or Woods: *Withe Sike*
dedicated to public use during a hurricane on 16 Oct 1902 in the presence of the sister of Edward VII, HRH Princess Louise

Co-founder of the NT, Canon Hardwicke Drummond Rawnsley, Vicar of Crosthwaite, Keswick – "The most active volcano in Europe" led the campaign to raise the funds and prevent development akin to Windermere's eastern shores.

OLD LEAD MINES
Brandlehow
Rupert's Wood
Bracken Burn

CHART II-N

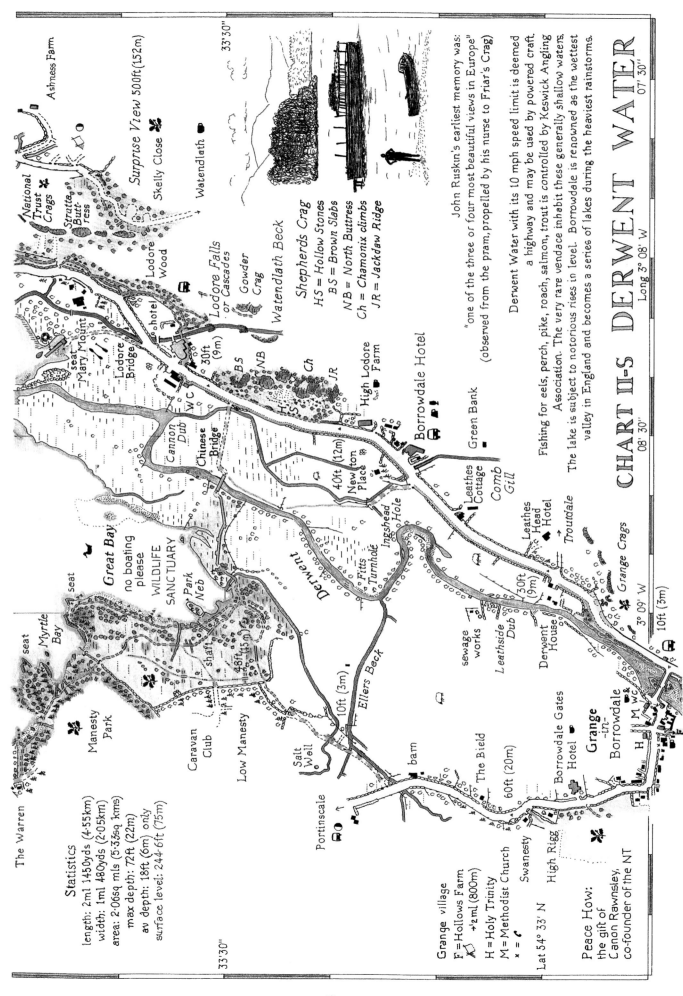

DERWENT WATER

CHART II·S

Long 3° 08' W

John Ruskin's earliest memory was: "one of the three or four most beautiful views in Europe" (observed from the pram, propelled by his nurse to Friar's Crag)

Derwent Water with its 10 mph speed limit is deemed a highway and may be used by powered craft.

Fishing for eels, perch, pike, roach, salmon, trout is controlled by Keswick Angling Association. The very rare vendace inhabit these generally shallow waters. Borrowdale is renowned as the wettest valley in England and becomes a series of lakes during the heaviest rainstorms.

Statistics
length: 2ml 1450yds (4·55km)
width: 1ml 480yds (2·05km)
area: 2·06sq mls (5·35sq kms)
max depth: 72ft (22m)
av depth: 18ft (6m) only
surface level: 244·6ft (75m)

Grange village
F = Hollows Farm →½ml (800m)
H = Holy Trinity
M = Methodist Church
× = ☎ Swanesty
Lat 54° 33' N

Peace How: the gift of Canon Rawnsley, co-founder of the NT

Shepherds Crag
HS = Hollow Stones
BS = Brown Slabs
NB = North Buttress
Ch = Chamonix climbs
JR = Jackdaw Ridge

Surprise View 500ft (152m)

Watendlath Beck

Lodore Falls or Cascades

Gowder Crag

National Trust Crags

Struttle Buttress

Skelly Close

Watendlath

Ashness Farm

The Warren

Myrtle Bay

Manesty Park

Great Bay
no boating please
WILDLIFE SANCTUARY

Park Neb

Caravan Club

Low Manesty

Salt Well

Portinscale

High Rigg

Grange-in-Borrowdale

Borrowdale Gates Hotel

The Bield

barn

sewage works

Leathside Dub

Derwent House

Troutdale

Grange Crags

Leathes Head Hotel

Leathes Cottage

Comb Gill

Green Bank

Borrowdale Hotel

High Lodore Farm

Newton Place

Ingshead Hole

Fitts Turnhole

Ellers Beck

Chinese Bridge

Cannon Dub

Mary Mount

Lodore Bridge

Lodore Wood

Lodore Hotel

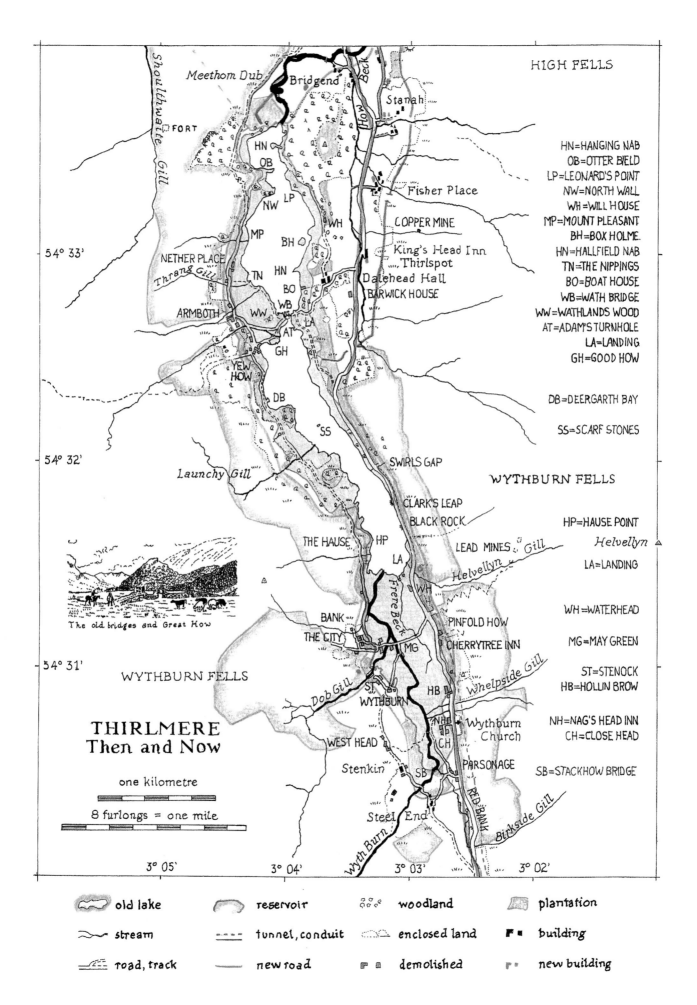

HIGH FELLS

Meethom Dub Bridgend *How Beck*

Stanah

Shoulthwaite Gill

FORT

HN

OB

Fisher Place

LP

COPPER MINE

NW

WH

King's Head Inn

MP

BH

Thirlspot

54° 33'

NETHER PLACE

Dalehead Hall

Thrang Gill

HN

BARWICK HOUSE

TN

BO

ARMBOTH

WB

WW

LA

AT

GH

YEW
HOW

DB

SS

54° 32'

Launchy Gill

SWIRLS GAP

WYTHBURN FELLS

CLARK'S LEAP

BLACK ROCK

HP=HAUSE POINT

THE HAUSE   HP

LEAD MINES *Helvellyn Gill*   *Helvellyn* △

Helvellyn

LA

LA=LANDING

Frere Beck

WH

WH=WATERHEAD

BANK

PINFOLD HOW

THE CITY

MG

CHERRYTREE INN

MG=MAY GREEN

54° 31'

WYTHBURN FELLS

ST=STENOCK

Dob Gill

ST

HB=HOLLIN BROW

WYTHBURN

HB

Whelpside Gill

NH

NH=NAG'S HEAD INN

WEST HEAD

CH

Wythburn
Church

CH=CLOSE HEAD

THIRLMERE
Then and Now

Stenkin

SB

PARSONAGE

SB=STACKHOW BRIDGE

one kilometre

RED BANK

8 furlongs = one mile

Steel End

Wyth Burn

Birkside Gill

3° 05'   3° 04'   3° 03'   3° 02'

HN=HANGING NAB
OB=OTTER BIELD
LP=LEONARD'S POINT
NW=NORTH WALL
WH=WILL HOUSE
MP=MOUNT PLEASANT
BH=BOX HOLME
HN=HALLFIELD NAB
TN=THE NIPPINGS
BO=BOAT HOUSE
WB=WATH BRIDGE
WW=WATHLANDS WOOD
AT=ADAM'S TURNHOLE
LA=LANDING
GH=GOOD HOW

DB=DEERGARTH BAY

SS=SCARF STONES

WYTHBURN FELLS

The old bridges and Great How

old lake   reservoir   woodland   plantation

stream   tunnel, conduit   enclosed land   building

road, track   new road   demolished   new building

72

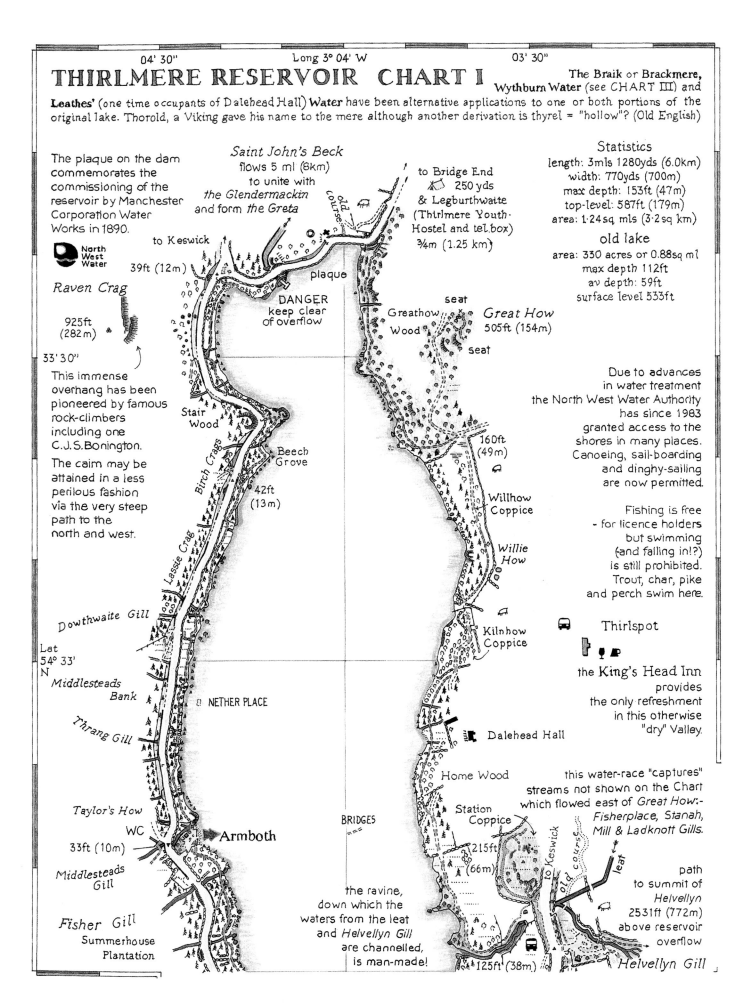

THIRLMERE RESERVOIR CHART I

The Braik or Brackmere, Wythburn Water (see CHART III) and **Leathes'** (one time occupants of Dalehead Hall) **Water** have been alternative applications to one or both portions of the original lake. Thorold, a Viking gave his name to the mere although another derivation is thyrel = "hollow"? (Old English)

Saint John's Beck flows 5 ml (8km) to unite with *the Glendermackin* and form *the Greta*

to Bridge End 🏕 250 yds & Legburthwaite (Thirlmere Youth Hostel and tel.box) ¾m (1.25 km)

The plaque on the dam commemorates the commissioning of the reservoir by Manchester Corporation Water Works in 1890.

North West Water

to Keswick

39ft (12m)

plaque

DANGER keep clear of overflow

seat
Greathow Wood
Great How 505ft (154m)
seat

Statistics
length: 3mls 1280yds (6.0km)
width: 770yds (700m)
max depth: 153ft (47m)
top-level: 587ft (179m)
area: 1·24sq mls (3·2sq km)

old lake
area: 330 acres or 0.88sq ml
max depth 112ft
av depth: 59ft
surface level 533ft

Raven Crag
925ft (282m)

33'30"

This immense overhang has been pioneered by famous rock-climbers including one C.J.S.Bonington.

The cairn may be attained in a less perilous fashion via the very steep path to the north and west.

Stair Wood

Birch Crags

Beech Grove
42ft (13m)

160ft (49m)

Due to advances in water treatment the North West Water Authority has since 1983 granted access to the shores in many places. Canoeing, sail-boarding and dinghy-sailing are now permitted.

Willhow Coppice

Willie How

Fishing is free - for licence holders but swimming (and falling in!?) is still prohibited. Trout, char, pike and perch swim here.

Lassie Crag

Dowthwaite Gill

Lat 54° 33' N

Middlesteads Bank

Thrang Gill

NETHER PLACE

Kilnhow Coppice

🚌 Thirlspot

the **King's Head Inn** provides the only refreshment in this otherwise "dry" Valley.

Dalehead Hall

Home Wood

this water-race "captures" streams not shown on the Chart which flowed east of *Great How*:- *Fisherplace, Stanah, Mill & Ladknott Gills.*

Taylor's How
WC
33ft (10m)

Station Coppice

215ft (66m)

to Keswick
old course
leat

BRIDGES

Middlesteads Gill

▲Armboth

path to summit of *Helvellyn* 2531ft (772m) above reservoir overflow

the ravine, down which the waters from the leat and *Helvellyn Gill* are channelled, is man-made!

Fisher Gill
Summerhouse Plantation

125ft (38m)

Helvellyn Gill

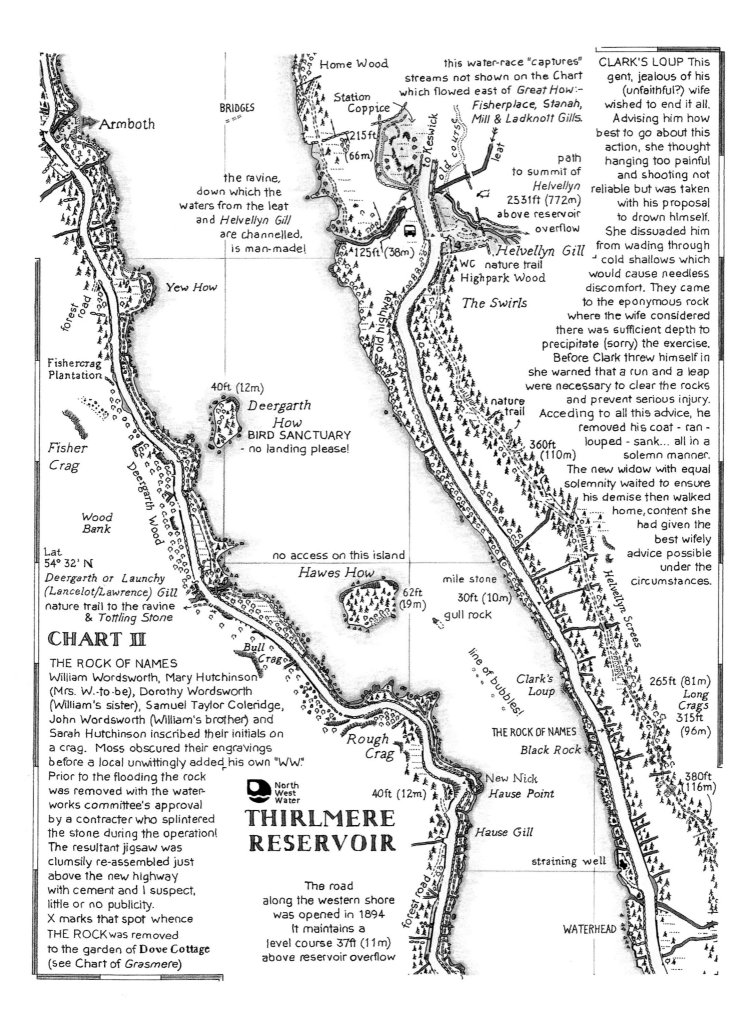

Armboth

Home Wood

this water-race "captures" streams not shown on the Chart which flowed east of *Great How*:— Fisherplace, Stanah, Mill & Ladknott Gills.

CLARK'S LOUP This gent, jealous of his (unfaithful?) wife wished to end it all. Advising him how best to go about this action, she thought hanging too painful and shooting not reliable but was taken with his proposal to drown himself. She dissuaded him from wading through cold shallows which would cause needless discomfort. They came to the eponymous rock where the wife considered there was sufficient depth to precipitate (sorry) the exercise. Before Clark threw himself in she warned that a run and a leap were necessary to clear the rocks and prevent serious injury. Acceding to all this advice, he removed his coat - ran - louped - sank... all in a solemn manner. The new widow with equal solemnity waited to ensure his demise then walked home, content she had given the best wifely advice possible under the circumstances.

BRIDGES

Station Coppice

215ft (66m)

to Keswick

old course

leat

path to summit of *Helvellyn* 2531ft (772m) above reservoir overflow

the ravine, down which the waters from the leat and *Helvellyn Gill* are channelled, is man-made!

125ft (38m)

Helvellyn Gill

WC nature trail Highpark Wood

The Swirls

Yew How

forest road

Fishercrag Plantation

40ft (12m)

Deergarth How BIRD SANCTUARY - no landing please!

Fisher Crag

Deergarth Wood

Wood Bank

nature trail

360ft (110m)

Lat 54° 32' N

Deergarth or Launchy (Lancelot/Lawrence) Gill nature trail to the ravine & *Tottling Stone*

no access on this island

Hawes How

62ft (19m)

mile stone

30ft (10m)

gull rock

Helvellyn Screes

CHART II

THE ROCK OF NAMES
William Wordsworth, Mary Hutchinson (Mrs. W.-to-be), Dorothy Wordsworth (William's sister), Samuel Taylor Coleridge, John Wordsworth (William's brother) and Sarah Hutchinson inscribed their initials on a crag. Moss obscured their engravings before a local unwittingly added his own "WW." Prior to the flooding the rock was removed with the water-works committee's approval by a contracter who splintered the stone during the operation! The resultant jigsaw was clumsily re-assembled just above the new highway with cement and I suspect, little or no publicity.
X marks that spot whence THE ROCK was removed to the garden of **Dove Cottage** (see Chart of *Grasmere*)

Bull Crag

line of bubbles!

Clark's Loup

265ft (81m) Long Crags 315ft (96m)

THE ROCK OF NAMES

Black Rock

Rough Crag

North West Water

THIRLMERE RESERVOIR

40ft (12m)

New Nick Hause Point

380ft (116m)

Hause Gill

straining well

The road along the western shore was opened in 1894 It maintains a level course 37ft (11m) above reservoir overflow

forest road

WATERHEAD

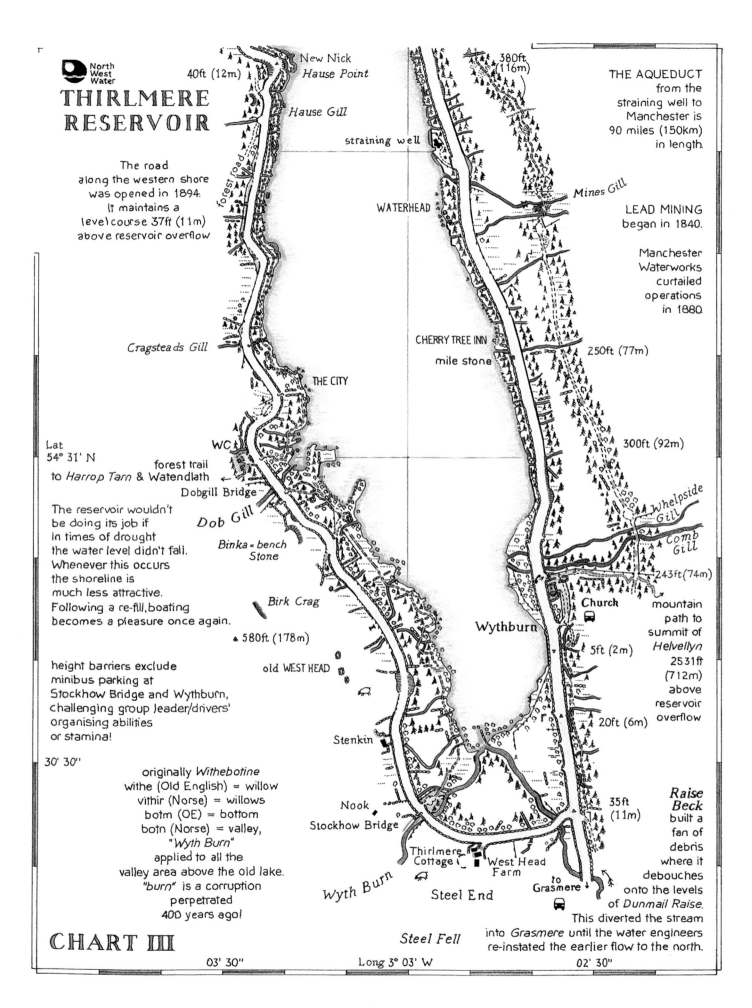

North West Water

THIRLMERE RESERVOIR

40ft (12m)

New Nick
Hause Point

Hause Gill

straining well

380ft (116m)

THE AQUEDUCT
from the straining well to Manchester is 90 miles (150km) in length.

forest road

WATERHEAD

The road along the western shore was opened in 1894. It maintains a level course 37ft (11m) above reservoir overflow

Mines Gill

LEAD MINING began in 1840.

Manchester Waterworks curtailed operations in 1880.

Cragsteads Gill

THE CITY

CHERRY TREE INN

mile stone

250ft (77m)

300ft (92m)

Lat 54° 31' N

WC

forest trail to *Harrop Tarn* & Watendlath ←

Dobgill Bridge

Dob Gill

Whelpside Gill

Comb Gill

The reservoir wouldn't be doing its job if in times of drought the water level didn't fall. Whenever this occurs the shoreline is much less attractive. Following a re-fill, boating becomes a pleasure once again.

Binka = bench Stone

243ft (74m)

Church

Birk Crag

▲ 580ft (178m)

old WEST HEAD

Wythburn

mountain path to summit of *Helvellyn* 2531ft (712m) above reservoir overflow

5ft (2m)

height barriers exclude minibus parking at Stockhow Bridge and Wythburn, challenging group leader/drivers' organising abilities or stamina!

20ft (6m)

30' 30"

Stenkin

originally *Withebotine* withe (Old English) = willow vithir (Norse) = willows botm (OE) = bottom botn (Norse) = valley, *"Wyth Burn"* applied to all the valley area above the old lake. *"burn"* is a corruption perpetrated 400 years ago!

Nook

Stockhow Bridge

Thirlmere Cottage

West Head Farm

35ft (11m)

Raise Beck built a fan of debris where it debouches onto the levels of *Dunmail Raise.* This diverted the stream into *Grasmere* until the water engineers re-instated the earlier flow to the north.

Wyth Burn

Steel End

to Grasmere

CHART III

Steel Fell

THIRLMERE: When Manchester Corporation Water Works converted the lake, the level was raised successively by 20 then 30 or so feet. The view down Saint John's Vale from Station Coppice to Blencathra is striking. I suppose that, had he the freedom we enjoy today, Wainwright would have included the ascent of Great How in his *Pictorial Guides to the Lakeland Fells*. The hill is a shapely, independent, thousand-footer dominating the foot of the water with a half-wooded, heathery top sporting an ancient heap of stones collected by contemporaries of William Wordsworth. Until the engineers transformed the valley, the Narrows were bridged by rickety planks linking drystone buttresses. Proposals were made to replace the old crossing with a ferry. The Justice or Steading Stone, site of the local "parliament", was submerged. Above the site The Cop, Rocking or Tottle Stone is Thirlmere's answer to the Bowder Stone in Borrowdale. Thirlmere used not to be as "dry". The King's Head Inn which lies outwith the catchment area has survived. The Nag's Head (this more vernacular appendage had replaced "The Horse's Head"), across the highway from Wythburn's Church, was closed and demolished many years after the damming of the lake. The Cherry Tree Inn, not a mile distant, was pulled down straight away as the site would be inundated.

The range and scale of forestry operations by North West Water and their predecessors almost overwhelms the catchment area. The old, straight boundaries are disappearing and a wider variety of species are planted. Several interesting trails with explanatory notes were established thirty years ago.

Wythburn Church has no dedicatory saint. The window in the west wall portrays Saint Cuthbert with the head of Saint Oswald. By the telephone box a stone tablet records that the poet Matthew Arnold (1822-88) commenced two rather lengthy walks from the church. On the first occasion his father, Doctor Thomas Arnold, headmaster of Rugby, led the ten-year-old boy and his elder girl across the fells to the sea on the west Cumbrian coast. Ten years later the siblings repeated the feat and Matthew immortalised their achievement with an epic poem.

While I was involved in the field examination of the Ordnance Survey 1:10,000 plans during the 1970s, I purchased a copy of the *Notes of Interest to Visitors* at Wythburn Church. The pamphlet mentioned the botched "transfer" of The Rock of Names to a position along the new road on the eastern side of the lake. As a book in my collection included its photograph, I recognised the insignificant assembly of flinty fragments while combing the indicated area. I positioned it on the field document and after some soul-searching and consultation reckoned a dot, annotated "cairn", would be the appropriate means of recording it for posterity without inviting the kind of vandalism beginning to infiltrate the remoter areas of the Lake District. Until the 80's I would point out the "Rock" and recount my discovery. Then I began to doubt my sense of geography as I continually failed to identify the spot for fellow-travellers. Watching the television, of all things, eventually reinstated my self-esteem. A local news programme featuring the re-furbished Wordsworth Museum at Town End, Grasmere, revealed the precious fragments were to be re-assembled in the garden of Dove Cottage. The latest-1998 print of the Outdoor Leisure Map has deleted the feature.

Dunmail, King of the British Kingdom of Strathclyde, defeated King Edmund of England at a battle in 945 or 946 AD. "They say" his remains lie beneath the massive cairn at the summit of the road, known as Dunmail Raise, on the boundary between Cumberland and Westmorland. Possibly a tumulus stood there a thousand or more years before that conflict. A thousand years after, navvies augmented the pile while tidying-up after the engineering of the Thirlmere Aqueduct. Dunmail's death (in Rome) was recorded thirty years later than his legendary demise. Ponder this: Dun (Gaelic), Maol (Welsh) and Raise (Norse) each mean "heap of stones"!

BROTHERS WATER, not quite the tiniest of the seventeen lakes, cannot be ignored by tourists crossing Lakeland's highest road, Kirkstone Pass. On the descent from the inn, Red Pit car park on the left affords the opportunity to photograph, paint, sketch or simply admire the water's classic setting of mountain and meadow. Hartsop-above-How's population once equalled or exceeded its sister township, Patterdale-below-How. While the slate quarries and mines in Hayeswater Gill and above Hartsop Hall were in operation, many hands were required to extract the lead ore with its traces of gold, silver and zinc. Some mines were worked until the 1930s. Nowadays their shafts and tunnels are death-traps. People who emerge unscathed are led by experienced, well-equipped specialists armed with local knowledge.

BROTHERS WATER

The old and descriptive "Broad/Broader Water" lost favour
following the drowning on New Year's Day c.1812 of two siblings.
The boys met their fate skating on the thin ice caused by springs
flowing from the bed of the Lake.   Water derives from
the Old English *waeter* or Norse *vatn*, meaning in this case lake.

Statistics
length: 860yds (780m)
width: 477yds (430m)
max depth: 50ft (15m)
surface level: 520ft (158m)

Lat
54° 31'
N

The inclusion of this small sheet of water in a list of the *"Lakes"*
is open to debate. What criteria should be applied?
When does a *tarn* become a *lake*?
Some guidebooks omit this, the smallest example, from listings.

Primary concerns are character and environment rather
than dimension. An extensive sheet of water occupying
a level, mainly pastoral setting might be considered a *lake*,
wheras one in a mountainous or elevated situation
is usually regarded as a *tarn*.

One *tarn* at least- Devoke *Water*, surpasses Brothers Water in area.
Although *water* translates into either *lake* or *tarn*,
tarns are always *tarns* and *meres* always *LAKES!*

Further vindication of Brothers Water's inclusion in this book:-
W.G. Collingwood referred to our subject as "that Lake".
It features in W. Heaton Cooper's *The Lakes*.
Ecologists make their distinction on biological grounds.

Although the rights of way follow virtually motorable
routes they are classified as footpaths
and not bridleways. Therefore....
NO RIDING.
Neither does the National Trust permit boating,
though trout-fishing is free. So....
NO CANOEING, please.

However the walk is a level, two-miles-
and-a-bit circuit enclosing the full
extent of the Lake's old glacial basin.
Since the ice receded debris
carried by four becks has filled
the hollow below the farms of
Hartsop Hall and Sykeside,
halving the original acreage of the Lake.

The mountains pitch steeply along the valley sides,
restricting the views. Kirkstone Pass with High Hartsop Dodd
to the South and Angletarn Pikes with Place Fell
in the opposite direction appear to advantage from these shores.

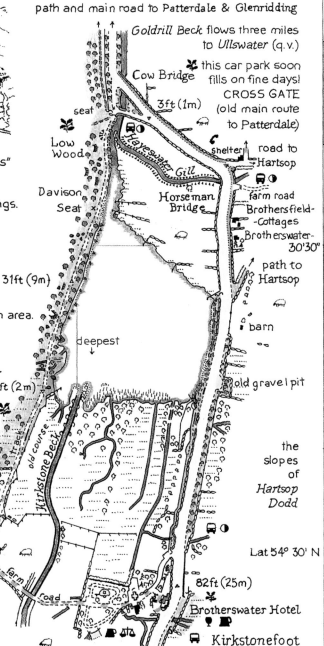

path and main road to Patterdale & Glenridding

Goldrill Beck flows three miles
to *Ullswater* (q.v.)

Cow Bridge

this car park soon
fills on fine days!
CROSS GATE
(old main route
to Patterdale)

seat   3ft (1m)

Low
Wood   shelter   road to
                                                   Hartsop
Davison
Seat   farm road
                        Horseman   Brothersfield
                        Bridge   -Cottages
                                                   Brotherswater-
                                                   30'30"
31ft (9m)   path to
                                                   Hartsop

                                                   barn
deepest

7ft (2m)   old gravel pit

                                                   the
                                                   slopes
                                                   of
                                                   *Hartsop
                                                   Dodd*

historic
Hartsop   Lat 54° 30' N
Hall
to   82ft (25m)
Dovedale
                                                   Brotherswater Hotel

                                                   Kirkstonefoot
Sykeside

main road over Kirkstone Pass
(Lakeland's highest road at 1489 ft)
to Ambleside and Windermere town

ULLSWATER is "The happiest combination of beauty and grandeur....." and "No lake can show such a varied margin and none (is) so interesting in its formation." -W.G.Collingwood.

Statistically Ullswater is a consistent "runner-up" of England's lakes. Totalling the score might give it top place. The three contrasting reaches are so varied and rewarding, no one can deny the appeal of Ullswater to holiday makers, tourists or adventurers. The mighty ranges of Helvellyn and High Street form dramatic backdrops and isolate the lake.

By tradition the Irish saint performed acts of baptism in the well at Patterdale. Alas, the Patrick whose name was ascribed to the valley in the 12th Century was more likely an Irish-Norseman of a later date. At the head and foot of the lake lie accommodating villages that cater to the needs of locals and visitors. No blatant retail therapy centres here.

The Ullswater Steamer service is a terrific facility. The one excursion many folk would recommend a first-time visitor to the Lake District is the sail to Howtown from Glenridding Pier, leaving the rest of the day for the return on foot along the shore beneath Hallin and Place Fells. From Easter to the end of October two to nine return sailings are made daily, according to season and Bank Holidays. Rowing boats, motor-boats, canoes and sailing boats are on hire at Glenridding, Pooley Bridge and Watermillock. The 10 m.p.h. speed limit ensures power boating and water-skiing won't disturb a day spent on, near, or by the water.

Weather and lake surface conditions are subject to tremendous contrast. The mountains slope directly to the water, creating downdraughts and turbulence which catch the unwary. Prevailing winds concentrate to produce alarmingly high waves and breakers along the open stretches. The eastern, pastoral Reach may bask in the sunshine, which the favoured Eden valley often enjoys, while the Helvellyn fells above the Patterdale Reach gather and hold heavy cloud during uncertain periods. In 1927 the delta of Glenridding Beck was violently augmented when Keppel Cove's dam burst, during heavy rain. Vast amounts of debris were washed into the lake.

The Mounsey family were voted Kings of Patterdale when they repulsed Scots raiders in 1648. The battle was fought on the "pass" above Stybarrow Crag - the present roadway was blasted out above the waterline much later. Their title was relinquished in 1825 when their alloted "palace", Patterdale Hall, was sold to the Marshall family. The lead mines of Glen Ridding originated under the very summit of Helvellyn at the end of the 1700s. Long tunnels and very deep shafts were excavated at lower and lower levels to extract tremendous quantities of ore until the closure of the Greenside Mine in 1960.

Tunnelling operations did not cease with the closure of the lead mines. The mountains and moors between Ullswater, Haweswater Reservoir and the major treatment plant north of Kendal have been pierced to allow controlled extraction of water.

HAWESWATER RESERVOIR: The flooding of Mardale during the Second World War is still lamented by many evacuees alive today. Life at the end of the millennium is more comfortable, less desperate than it was during the times of economic recession and world conflict which pertained during the building of the dam. Such domestic and social disruption allied to conservationists' objections is leading the industry to employ new technologies to meet increases in the demand for water during the 21st Century.

Long-distance walkers bound for the North Sea descend from Kidsty Pike to the ruins of Riggingdale, traverse the western "tide-line" and, crossing old Naddle Bridge, follow a depleted Mardale Beck beyond the margins of our Charts to bid farewell to The Lakes.

Kidsty Pike
and the
Haweswater Dam
from the East

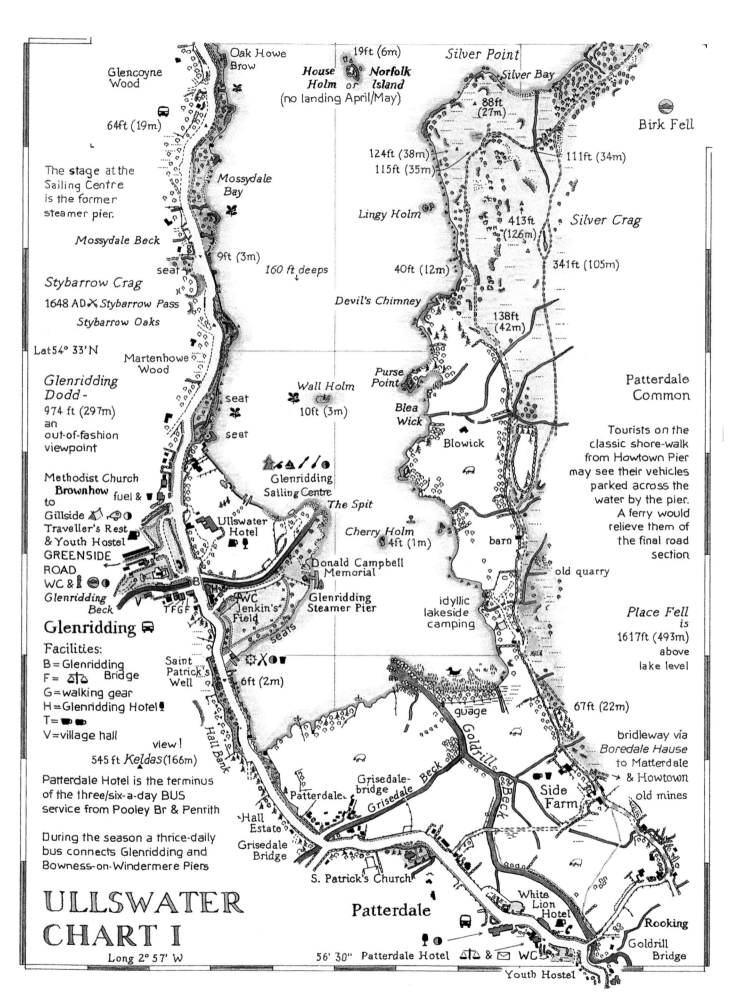

ULLSWATER CHART II-W

"Airey" was the favoured
spelling until the 1930s
isara (Celtic) = strong river
eyr- á (Norse) = gravel-banked + stream
ergo: Beck from *bekke* (Norse) is a tautology

Aira Force: the scene of a tragedy immortalised
by Wordsworth in his poem "The Somnambulist".
A maiden, distressed by rumours of her lover's death in battle,
has taken to sleep-walking above her abode, Lyulph's Tower.
The knight, home from the Crusades, returned directly
to their tryst, finds her standing above the abyss.
Her entranced state and his gentle touch causes her
to overbalance and plunge into the chasm
where his heroic efforts fail to revive her.

The BRIDGES were built in memory of three brothers- Stephen
(who died in 1902), Cecil (1919) and Gerald (1916) - of the Spring Rice
family who lived on these shores and enjoyed marital connections with
the Marshalls of Patterdale. A tablet, inscribed in remembrance of
the ambassador/poet Sir Cecil, is set into the parapet of the lower bridge.

DONALD CAMPBELL pushed the World Water Speed Record
over the 200 mph barrier during 1955 on this lake.
Momentos of this event are displayed in the
Glenridding Hotel, his base for the attempts.
The slate memorial at Glenridding Pier
was unveiled in 1997.
refer to CHART I

Sister Dorothy's Journal (1802) notes
the actual location of the profusion
of *narcissi* (wild daff's)
celebrated in William Wordsworth's
- indeed *anybody's* -
most-quoted poetry piece.

Lat 54° 34' N

the
parish boundary
of Matterdale in
old Cumberland &
Patterdale in old
Westmorland
follows
*Glencoyne
Beck*
↓

to *High Force*

180ft (55 m)   *Aira Force*

to *Yew Crag*

Victorian glade

Aira Beck

WC

to Dockray
& Keswick
PARK BROW

Groovegill Beck

*Aira
Green*

tourists once
visited *Aira Force*
by steamer

Aira Point

Glencoyne Park

Far-

-Swan Becks

Middle-

Near-

deepest here
↓
205ft (63m)

Ewe Crag

18ft (6m)

Glencoyne
Bridge

Glencoyne Beck

↑

Glen Coyne

4ft (1m)

Oak Howe
Brow

19ft (6m)

Silver Point

Silver Bay

Birkfell Earth

"earth"
=
foxes'
lairs

Glencoyne
Wood

House   **Norfolk**
Holm or **Island**
(no landing April/May)

88ft
(27m)

64ft (19m)

Birk Fell

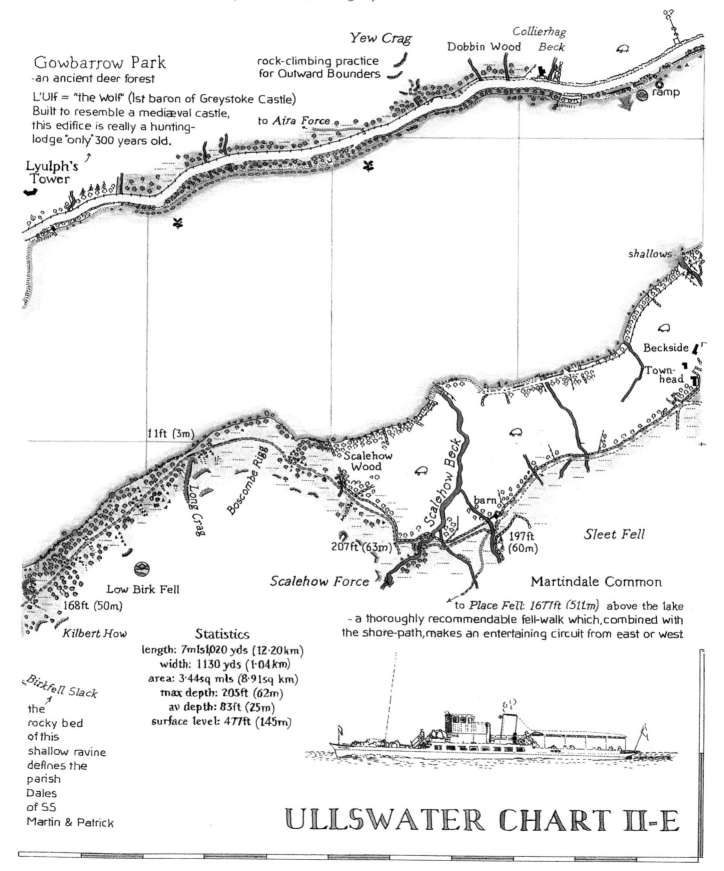

An early spelling was Ulveswater. Ulf's Lake. Ulf or Wolf (see below)
plus water derived from "vatn" (Norse) and waeter (Old English)

Gowbarrow Park
-an ancient deer forest

L'Ulf = "the Wolf" (1st baron of Greystoke Castle)
Built to resemble a mediæval castle,
this edifice is really a hunting-
lodge "only" 300 years old.

Lyulph's Tower

Yew Crag

rock-climbing practice
for Outward Bounders

to *Aira Force*

Dobbin Wood

Collierhag Beck

ramp

shallows

Beckside

Town-head

11ft (3m)

Long Crag

Boscombe Rigg

Scalehow Wood

Scalehow Beck

barn

Low Birk Fell

168ft (50m)

Kilbert How

207ft (63m)

Scalehow Force

197ft (60m)

Sleet Fell

Martindale Common

to *Place Fell: 1677ft (511m)* above the lake
- a thoroughly recommendable fell-walk which, combined with
the shore-path, makes an entertaining circuit from east or west

Birkfell Slack

the
rocky bed
of this
shallow ravine
defines the
parish
Dales
of SS
Martin & Patrick

Statistics
length: 7mls 1,020 yds (12·20km)
width: 1130 yds (1·04km)
area: 3·44sq mls (8·91sq km)
max depth: 205ft (62m)
av depth: 83ft (25m)
surface level: 477ft (145m)

ULLSWATER CHART II-E

ULLSWATER CHART III-W

schelly

Forty years ago the water authorities planned to convert Ullswater to a reservoir! LORD BIRKETT took on the legal battle which culminated in a debate where his eloquence won over the majority of his fellow peers in the Upper House. The enormous struggle cost him his life. In 1962 Norman Birkett died only two days after a famous victory. Water has since been extracted and pumped up to Haweswater Reservoir through a tunnel - but without loss to the superb sporting and visual amenity of the lake. His campaigning efforts were recognised when *Nameless Fell* on the northern range of *Helvellyn* was re-titled *Birkett Fell.* The Birkett Plaque fixed to *Kailpot Crag* on the southern shore may be read by swimmers, boatmen and rock-climbers with sticky boots.

For licence holders, FISHING may result in landing char, perch, trout and the elusive, long, silvery skelly/schelly, or gwyniad- which must be returned. These denizens of the deep only inhabited *Red Tarn*, *(Helvellyn)* & *Hawes Water.* In olden times nets, stretched between *SKELLY Nab* and *Geordie's Crag,* intercepted cart-loads of char and schelly migrating between the basins of the middle and eastern reaches.

The laybys along the northern shore are places for the car-bound to relax and contemplate.

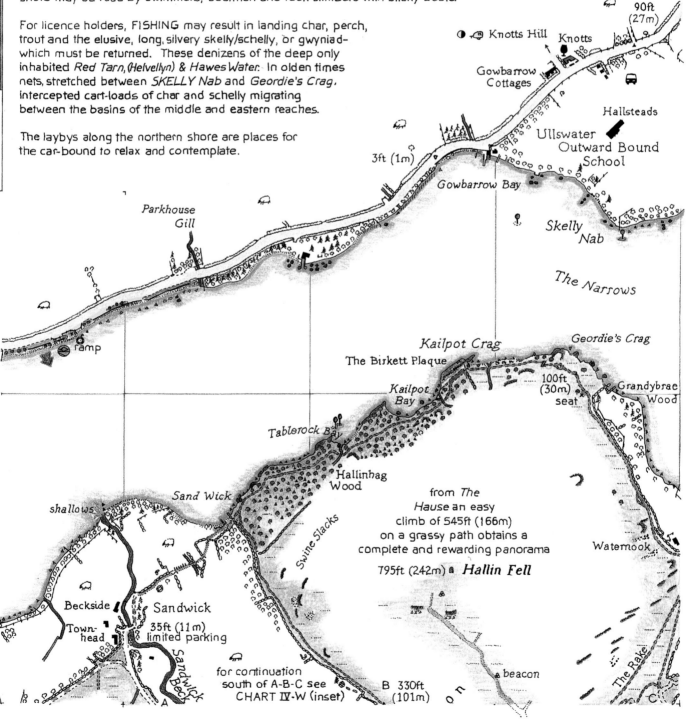

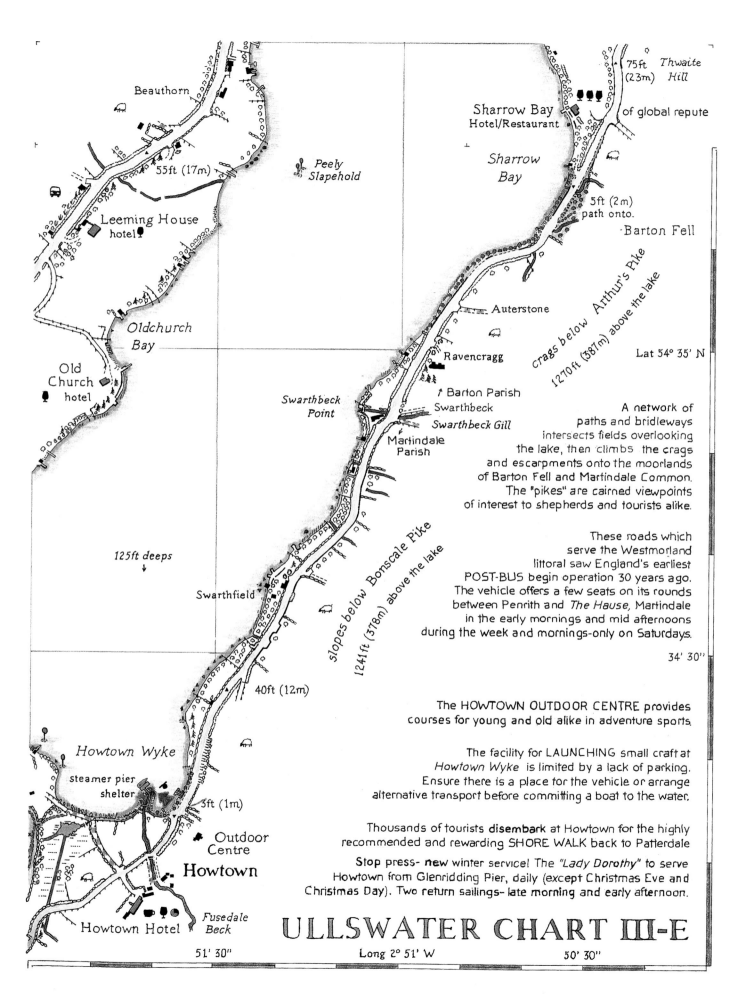

Beauthorn

75ft (23m) *Thwaite Hill*

Sharrow Bay
Hotel/Restaurant
of global repute

55ft (17m)

Peely Slapehold

Sharrow Bay

Leeming House hotel

5ft (2m) path onto

Barton Fell

Oldchurch Bay

Auterstone

Old Church hotel

Ravencragg

↑ Barton Parish
Swarthbeck
Swarthbeck Gill

Swarthbeck Point

Martindale Parish

crags below Arthur's Pike
1270ft (387m) above the lake

Lat 54° 35' N

A network of
paths and bridleways
intersects fields overlooking
the lake, then climbs the crags
and escarpments onto the moorlands
of Barton Fell and Martindale Common.
The "pikes" are cairned viewpoints
of interest to shepherds and tourists alike.

These roads which
serve the Westmorland
littoral saw England's earliest
POST-BUS begin operation 30 years ago.
The vehicle offers a few seats on its rounds
between Penrith and *The Hause*, Martindale
in the early mornings and mid afternoons
during the week and mornings-only on Saturdays.

34' 30"

125ft deeps ↓

Swarthfield

slopes below Bonscale Pike
1241ft (378m) above the lake

40ft (12m)

The HOWTOWN OUTDOOR CENTRE provides
courses for young and old alike in adventure sports.

The facility for LAUNCHING small craft at
Howtown Wyke is limited by a lack of parking.
Ensure there is a place for the vehicle or arrange
alternative transport before committing a boat to the water.

Howtown Wyke

steamer pier shelter

3ft (1m)

Outdoor Centre

Howtown

Howtown Hotel

Fusedale Beck

Thousands of tourists **disembark** at Howtown for the highly
recommended and rewarding SHORE WALK back to Patterdale

Stop press- new winter service! The *"Lady Dorothy"* to serve
Howtown from Glenridding Pier, daily (except Christmas Eve and
Christmas Day). Two return sailings- late morning and early afternoon.

ULLSWATER CHART III-E

51' 30"

Long 2° 51' W

50' 30"

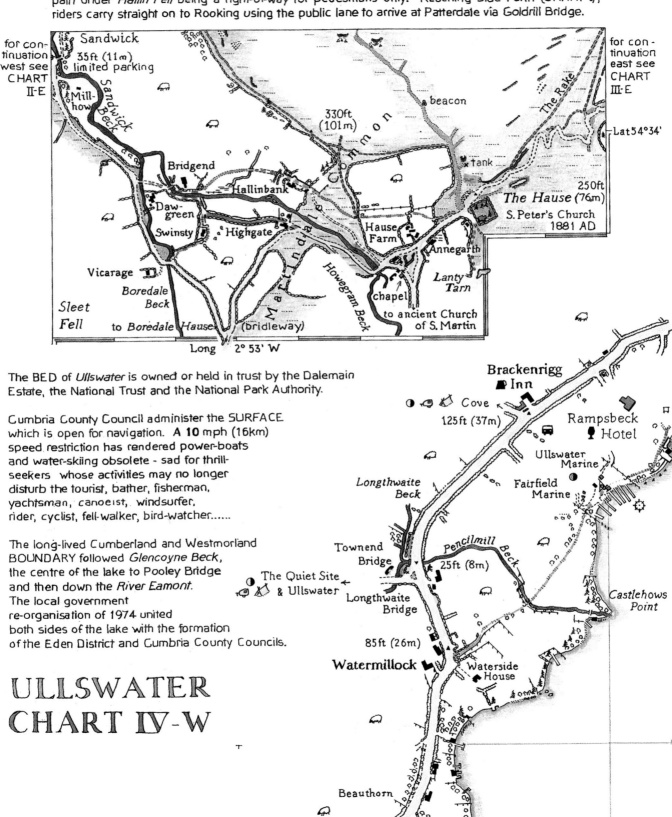

This INSET of **MARTINDALE** is appended for the benefit of RIDERS wishing to follow the southern shore from Pooley Bridge to Patterdale or indeed make a complete circuit of the lake, the path under *Hallin Fell* being a right-of-way for pedestrians only.   Reaching Side Farm (CHART I), riders carry straight on to Rooking using the public lane to arrive at Patterdale via Goldrill Bridge.

for con-
tinuation
west see
CHART
II·E

Sandwick
35ft (11m)
limited parking

Mill-
how

Sandwick Beck

Bridgend

Hallinbank

Daw-
green

Swinsty

Highgate

Vicarage

Boredale
Beck

Sleet
Fell

to Boredale House   (bridleway)

Martindale Common

330ft
(101m)

beacon

The Rake

tank

Hause
Farm

Howegran Beck

chapel

Annegarth

Lanty
Tarn

to ancient Church
of S. Martin

for con-
tinuation
east see
CHART
III·E

Lat 54°34'

250ft
The Hause (76m)
S. Peter's Church
1881 AD

Long 2° 53' W

The BED of *Ullswater* is owned or held in trust by the Dalemain Estate, the National Trust and the National Park Authority.

Cumbria County Council administer the SURFACE which is open for navigation. A **10** mph (16km) speed restriction has rendered power-boats and water-skiing obsolete - sad for thrill-seekers whose activities may no longer disturb the tourist, bather, fisherman, yachtsman, canoeist, windsurfer, rider, cyclist, fell-walker, bird-watcher......

The long-lived Cumberland and Westmorland BOUNDARY followed *Glencoyne Beck*, the centre of the lake to Pooley Bridge and then down the *River Eamont*. The local government re-organisation of 1974 united both sides of the lake with the formation of the Eden District and Cumbria County Councils.

ULLSWATER
CHART IV-W

Brackenrigg
Inn

Cove
125ft (37m)

Rampsbeck
Hotel

Ullswater
Marine

Longthwaite
Beck

Fairfield
Marine

Townend
Bridge

Pencilmill Beck

25ft (8m)

Castlehows
Point

The Quiet Site
& Ullswater

Longthwaite
Bridge

85ft (26m)

Watermillock

Waterside
House

Beauthorn

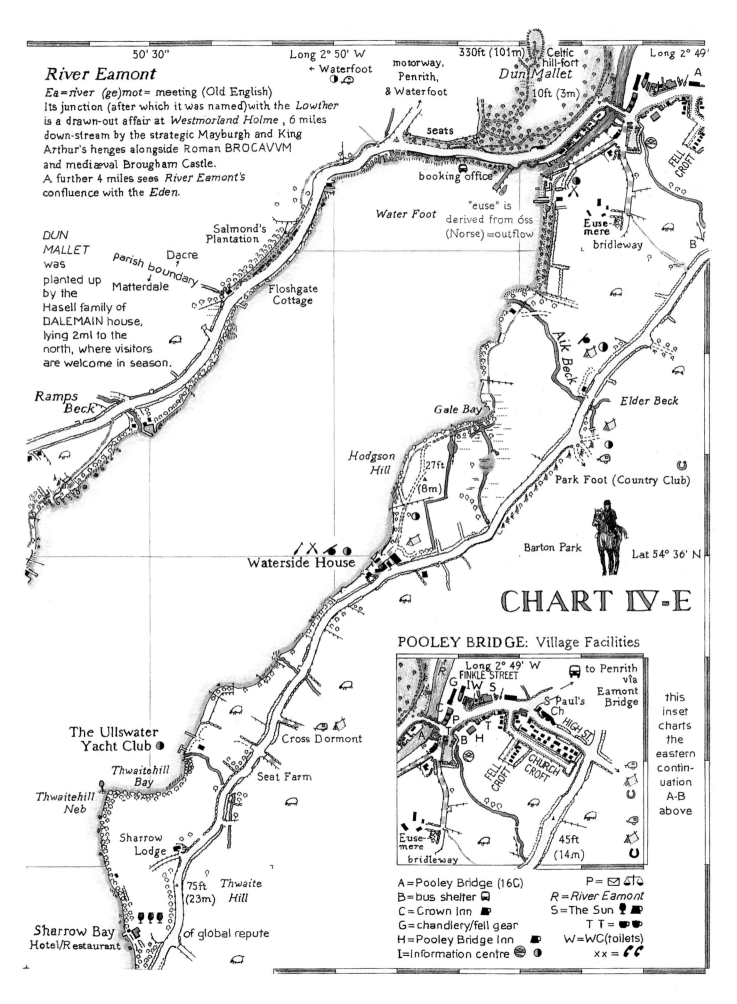

River Eamont

Ea = *river* *(ge)mot* = meeting (Old English)
Its junction (after which it was named) with the *Lowther*
is a drawn-out affair at *Westmorland Holme*, 6 miles
down-stream by the strategic Mayburgh and King
Arthur's henges alongside Roman BROCAVVM
and mediæval Brougham Castle.
A further 4 miles sees *River Eamont's*
confluence with the *Eden*.

DUN MALLET was planted up by the Hasell family of DALEMAIN house, lying 2ml to the north, where visitors are welcome in season.

Long 2° 50' W
← Waterfoot

motorway, Penrith, & Waterfoot

330ft (101m)   Celtic hill-fort
Dun Mallet
10ft (3m)

seats

booking office

Water Foot

"euse" is derived from óss (Norse) = outflow

Euse-mere bridleway

50' 30"   Long 2° 49'

A

FELL CROFT

B

Salmond's Plantation

Dacre
parish boundary
Matterdale

Floshgate Cottage

Aik Beck

Elder Beck

Ramps Beck

Gale Bay

Hodgson Hill
27ft (8m)

Park Foot (Country Club)

Barton Park

Lat 54° 36' N

CHART IV-E

Waterside House

The Ullswater Yacht Club ●

Thwaitehill Bay

Thwaitehill Neb

Cross Dormont

Seat Farm

POOLEY BRIDGE: Village Facilities

Long 2° 49' W
FINKLE STREET
I W S
G
C
P
A
B H
T

S Paul's Ch

to Penrith vîa Eamont Bridge

HIGH ST.

FELL CROFT
CHURCH CROFT

Euse-mere bridleway

45ft (14m)

this inset charts the eastern contin-uation A-B above

Sharrow Lodge

75ft (23m)   *Thwaite Hill*

Sharrow Bay
Hotel/Restaurant

of global repute

A = Pooley Bridge (16C)
B = bus shelter
C = Crown Inn
G = chandlery/fell gear
H = Pooley Bridge Inn
I = Information centre

P = ✉ ⚖
R = *River Eamont*
S = The Sun
T T =
W = WC(toilets)
xx = ❝❞

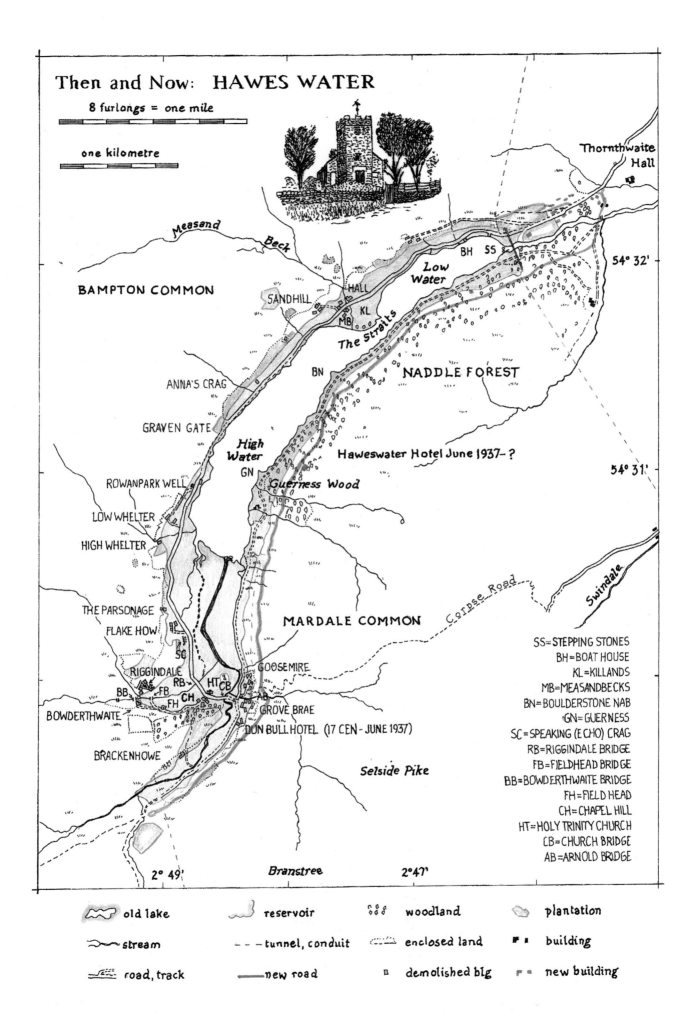

Then and Now: HAWES WATER

8 furlongs = one mile

one kilometre

Measand Beck

BAMPTON COMMON

SANDHILL

HALL
KL
MB

Low Water

BH SS

54° 32'

The Straits

BN

NADDLE FOREST

ANNA'S CRAG

GRAVEN GATE

High Water
GN

Haweswater Hotel June 1937-?

54° 31'

Guerness Wood

ROWANPARK WELL

LOW WHELTER

HIGH WHELTER

Corpse Road

Swindale

THE PARSONAGE

FLAKE HOW

SC

MARDALE COMMON

RIGGINDALE
RB
BB   FB   HT CB
      FH   CH   AB

GOOSEMIRE

BOWDERTHWAITE

GROVE BRAE

DUN BULL HOTEL (17 CEN - JUNE 1937)

BRACKENHOWE

Selside Pike

SS = STEPPING STONES
BH = BOAT HOUSE
KL = KILLANDS
MB = MEASANDBECKS
BN = BOULDERSTONE NAB
GN = GUERNESS
SC = SPEAKING (ECHO) CRAG
RB = RIGGINDALE BRIDGE
FB = FIELDHEAD BRIDGE
BB = BOWDERTHWAITE BRIDGE
FH = FIELD HEAD
CH = CHAPEL HILL
HT = HOLY TRINITY CHURCH
CB = CHURCH BRIDGE
AB = ARNOLD BRIDGE

2° 49'   Branstree   2° 47'

Thornthwaite Hall

old lake   reservoir   woodland   plantation

stream   --- tunnel, conduit   enclosed land   building

road, track   new road   demolished blg   new building

86

HAWESWATER RESERVOIR CHART I

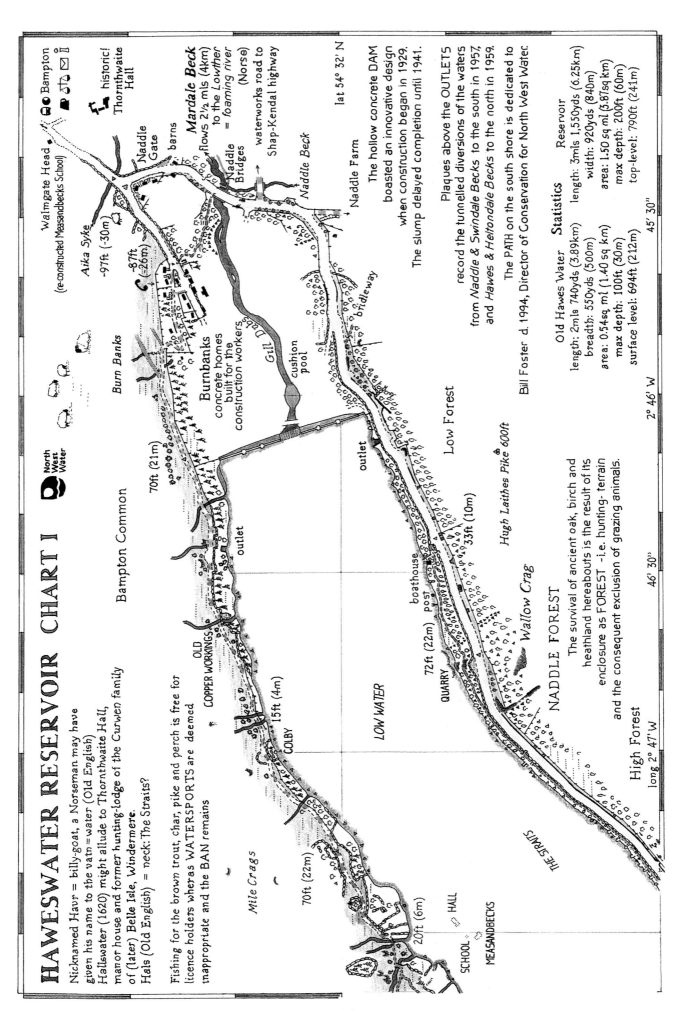

North West Water

Nicknamed Havr = billy-goat, a Norseman may have given his name to the vatn = water (Old English)
Hallswater (1620) might allude to Thornthwaite Hall, manor house and former hunting-lodge of the Curwen family of (later) Belle Isle, Windermere.
Hals (Old English) = neck: The Straits?

Fishing for the brown trout, char, pike and perch is free for licence holders whereas WATERSPORTS are deemed inappropriate and the BAN remains

Bampton
● Bampton
historic!
Thornthwaite Hall

Walmgate Head
(re-constructed Measandbecks School)

Aika Syke
-97ft (-30m)
-87ft (-26m)

Naddle Gate
barns

Naddle Bridges

Mardale Beck
flows 2½ mls (4km) to the Lowther = foaming river (Norse)
waterworks road to Shap-Kendal highway

Naddle Beck

lat 54° 32' N

Naddle Farm

The hollow concrete DAM boasted an innovative design when construction began in 1929. The slump delayed completion until 1941.

Plaques above the OUTLETS record the tunnelled diversions of the waters from Naddle & Swindale Becks to the south in 1957, and Hawes & Heltondale Becks to the north in 1959.

The PATH on the south shore is dedicated to Bill Foster d. 1994, Director of Conservation for North West Water.

Statistics

Old Hawes Water
length: 2mls 740yds (3.89km)
breadth: 550yds (500m)
area: 0.54sq ml (1.40 sq km)
max depth: 100ft (30m)
surface level: 694ft (212m)

Reservoir
length: 3mls 1,550yds (6.25km)
width: 920yds (840m)
area: 1.50 sq ml (3.87sq km)
max depth: 200ft (60m)
top-level: 790ft (241m)

2° 46' W
45' 30"

Burn Banks

70ft (21m)

Burnbanks concrete homes built for the construction workers

Gill Dub
cushion pool

outlet

bridleway

outlet

Low Forest

boathouse
POST

33ft (10m)

Hugh Laithes Pike 600ft

72ft (22m)

QUARRY

Wallow Crag

NADDLE FOREST

The survival of ancient oak, birch and heathland hereabouts is the result of its enclosure as FOREST -i.e. hunting- terrain and the consequent exclusion of grazing animals.

Bampton Common

Mile Crags

70ft (22m)

OLD COPPER WORKINGS

15ft (4m)

COLBY

LOW WATER

46' 30"

High Forest

long 2° 47' W

THE STRAITS

20ft (6m)

SCHOOL □ HALL

MEASANDBECKS

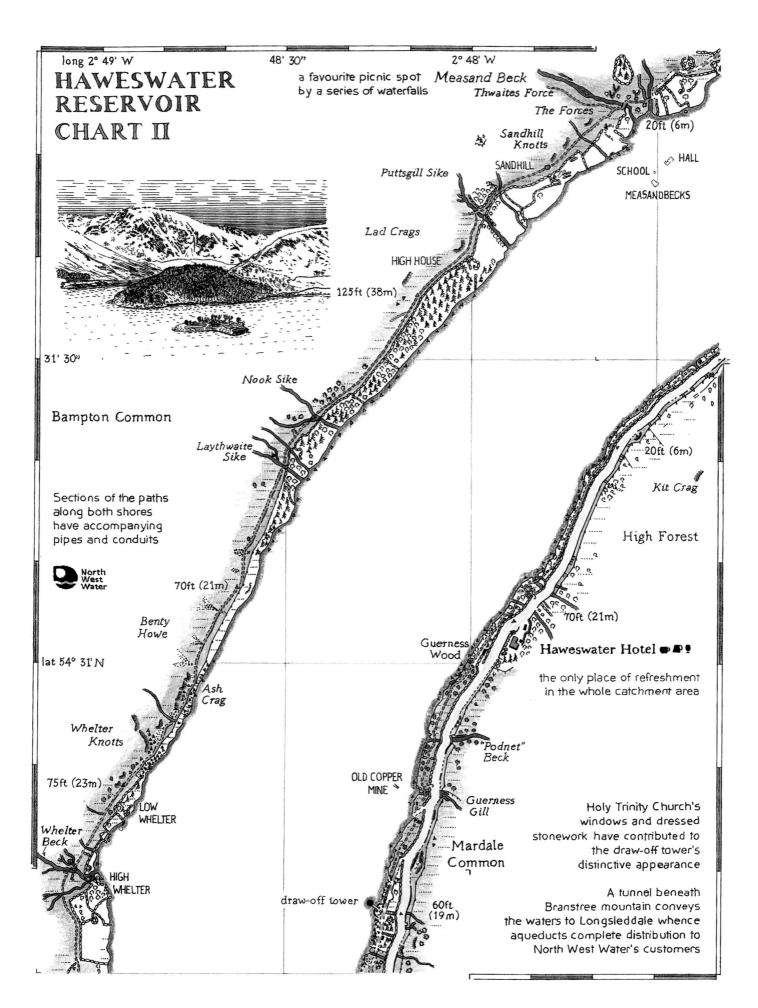

HAWESWATER RESERVOIR CHART II

long 2° 49' W

48' 30"

2° 48' W

a favourite picnic spot
by a series of waterfalls

Measand Beck

Thwaites Force

The Forces

20ft (6m)

Sandhill Knotts

SANDHILL

Puttsgill Sike

SCHOOL

HALL

MEASANDBECKS

Lad Crags

HIGH HOUSE

125ft (38m)

31' 30"

Bampton Common

Nook Sike

Laythwaite Sike

20ft (6m)

Kit Crag

High Forest

Sections of the paths
along both shores
have accompanying
pipes and conduits

North
West
Water

70ft (21m)

70ft (21m)

Benty Howe

Guerness Wood

Haweswater Hotel

the only place of refreshment
in the whole catchment area

lat 54° 31' N

Ash Crag

Whelter Knotts

"Podnet" Beck

75ft (23m)

LOW WHELTER

OLD COPPER MINE

Guerness Gill

Whelter Beck

HIGH WHELTER

Mardale Common

Holy Trinity Church's
windows and dressed
stonework have contributed to
the draw-off tower's
distinctive appearance

draw-off tower

60ft (19m)

A tunnel beneath
Branstree mountain conveys
the waters to Longsleddale whence
aqueducts complete distribution to
North West Water's customers

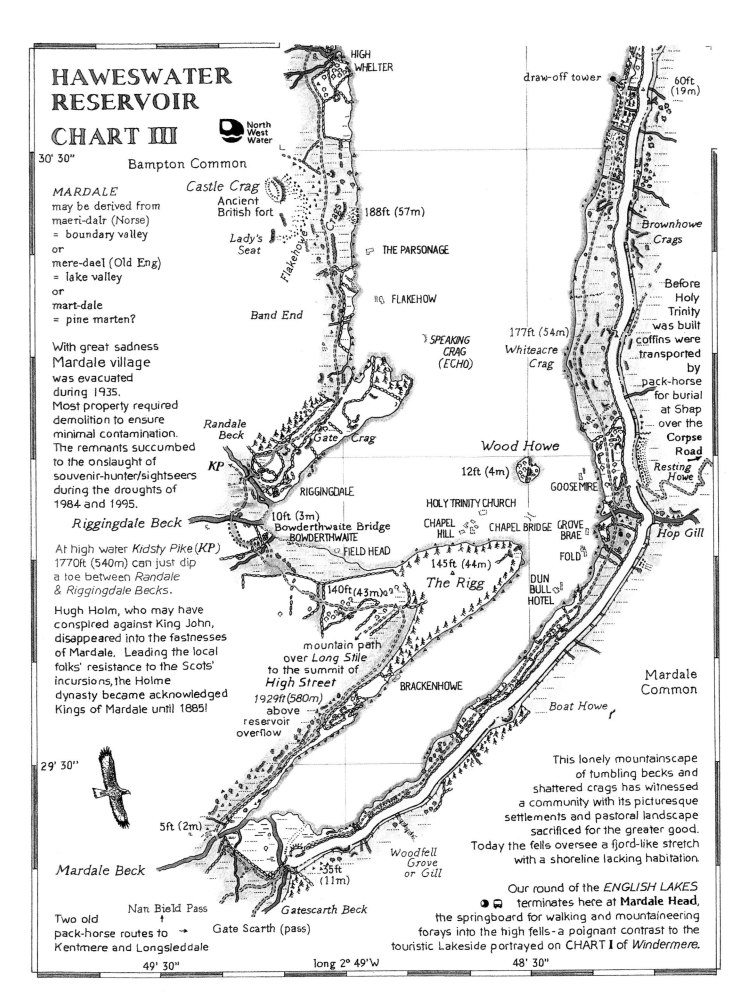

HAWESWATER RESERVOIR CHART III

North West Water

30' 30"

Bampton Common

MARDALE
may be derived from
maeri-dalr (Norse)
= boundary valley
or
mere-dael (Old Eng)
= lake valley
or
mart-dale
= pine marten?

With great sadness
Mardale village
was evacuated
during 1935.
Most property required
demolition to ensure
minimal contamination.
The remnants succumbed
to the onslaught of
souvenir-hunter/sightseers
during the droughts of
1984 and 1995.

Riggingdale Beck

At high water *Kidsty Pike (KP)*
1770ft (540m) can just dip
a toe between *Randale
& Riggingdale Becks.*

Hugh Holm, who may have
conspired against King John,
disappeared into the fastnesses
of Mardale. Leading the local
folks' resistance to the Scots'
incursions, the Holme
dynasty became acknowledged
Kings of Mardale until 1885!

29' 30"

5ft (2m)

Mardale Beck

Nan Bield Pass

Two old
pack-horse routes to
Kentmere and Longsleddale

Gate Scarth (pass)

Gatescarth Beck

35ft (11m)

*Woodfell
Grove
or Gill*

49' 30"

HIGH WHELTER

Castle Crag
Ancient
British fort

*Lady's
Seat*

Flakehowe Crags

188ft (57m)

THE PARSONAGE

FLAKEHOW

Band End

*SPEAKING
CRAG
(ECHO)*

*Randale
Beck*

Gate Crag

KP

RIGGINGDALE

10ft (3m)
Bowderthwaite Bridge
BOWDERTHWAITE

FIELD HEAD

140ft (43m)

145ft (44m)

The Rigg

mountain path
over *Long Stile*
to the summit of
High Street
1929ft (580m)
above
reservoir
overflow

BRACKENHOWE

draw-off tower

60ft (19m)

*Brownhowe
Crags*

177ft (54m)
*Whiteacre
Crag*

Wood Howe

12ft (4m)

HOLY TRINITY CHURCH

GOOSEMIRE

CHAPEL
HILL

CHAPEL BRIDGE

GROVE
BRAE

FOLD

DUN
BULL
HOTEL

Before
Holy
Trinity
was built
coffins were
transported
by
pack-horse
for burial
at Shap
over the
**Corpse
Road**

*Resting
Howe*

Hop Gill

Mardale
Common

Boat Howe

This lonely mountainscape
of tumbling becks and
shattered crags has witnessed
a community with its picturesque
settlements and pastoral landscape
sacrificed for the greater good.
Today the fells oversee a fjord-like stretch
with a shoreline lacking habitation.

Our round of the *ENGLISH LAKES*
● 🚌 terminates here at **Mardale Head**,
the springboard for walking and mountaineering
forays into the high fells - a poignant contrast to the
touristic Lakeside portrayed on CHART I of *Windermere.*

long 2° 49'W

48' 30"

STATISTICS

Although these dimensions are included on the CHARTS, these "League Tables" have been compiled for those interested in superlative or who appreciate lists.

	old Hawes Water		old Thirlmere	
Area	0·54	1·40	0·52	1·34
Length	2·42	3·89	2·67	4·30
Breadth	0·31	0·50	0·38	0·61
Alt.	694	212	533	162
Depth	100	30	112	34

LENGTH	miles	kms
Windermere	11·24	18·08
Ullswater	7·58	12·20
Coniston Water	5·39	8·30
Bassenthwaite Lake	3·90	6·28
Haweswater Reservoir	3·86	6·22
Thirlmere Reservoir	3·73	6·00
Wast Water	3·03	4·88
Derwent Water	2·82	4·55
Crummock Water	2·54	4·09
Ennerdale Water	2·40	3·86
Esthwaite Water	1·59	2·55
Buttermere	1·26	2·03
Lowes Water	1·03	1·66
Grasmere	0·95	1·54
Rydal Water	0·73	1·18
Elter Water	0·58	0·93
Brothers Water	0·49	0·78

ALTITUDE	feet	metres
Haweswater Reservoir	790	241
Thirlmere Reservoir	587	179
Brothers Water	520	158
Ullswater	477	145
Lowes Water	399	122
Ennerdale Water	370	113
Buttermere	330	101
Crummock Water	321	99
Derwent Water	244	75
Bassenthwaite Lake	224	69
Esthwaite Water	214	65
Grasmere	208	62
Wast Water	200	61
Elter Water	187	57
Rydal Water	177	54
Coniston Water	143	44
Windermere	128	39

AREA	sq miles	sq kms
Windermere	5·69	14·73
Ullswater	3·44	8·91
Bassenthwaite Lake	2·06	5·33
Derwent Water	2·06	5·33
Coniston Water	1·89	4·89
Haweswater Reservoir	1·50	3·87
Thirlmere Reservoir	1·24	3·21
Wast Water	1·12	2·90
Ennerdale Water	1·12	2·90
Crummock Water	0·97	2·51
Esthwaite Water	0·37	0·96
Buttermere	0·36	0·93
Lowes Water	0·24	0·63
Grasmere	0·24	0·62
Rydal Water	0·12	0·31
Brothers Water	0·07	0·19
Elter Water	0·06	0·15

BREADTH	miles	kms
Derwent Water	1·27	2·05
Windermere	0·93	1·49
Bassenthwaite Lake	0·80	1·28
Ennerdale Water	0·65	1·04
Ullswater	0·64	1·03
Crummock Water	0·62	1·00
Haweswater Reservoir	0·52	0·84
Coniston Water	0·49	0·79
Wast Water	0·48	0·78
Thirlmere Reservoir	0·44	0·71
Grasmere	0·40	0·64
Buttermere	0·37	0·60
Esthwaite Water	0·37	0·59
Lowes Water	0·35	0·56
Brothers Water	0·27	0·43
Rydal Water	0·22	0·35
Elter Water	0·20	0·32

DEPTH	feet	metres
Wast Water	258	79
Windermere	219	67
Ullswater	205	62
Haweswater Reservoir	200	61
Coniston Water	184	56
Thirlmere Reservoir	153	47
Ennerdale Water	148	45
Crummock Water	144	44
Buttermere	94	28
Derwent Water	72	22
Bassenthwaite Lake	70	19
Grasmere	70	19
Rydal Water	56	17
Lowes Water	53	16
Brothers Water	50	15
Esthwaite Water	47	14
Elter Water	20	6

GEOLOGY AND FORMER LAKE EXTENTS

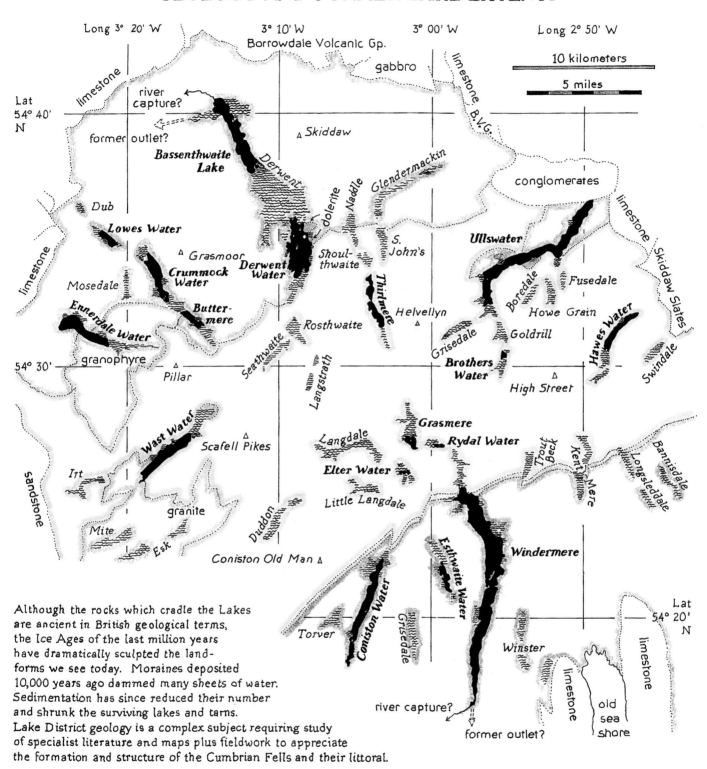

Long 3° 20' W
3° 10' W
Borrowdale Volcanic Gp.
3° 00' W
Long 2° 50' W

gabbro

10 kilometers

5 miles

Lat 54° 40' N

limestone

river capture?

former outlet?

Bassenthwaite Lake

△ Skiddaw

Derwent

limestone B.V.G.

Glendermackin

conglomerates

limestone

Dub

Lowes Water

△ Grasmoor

dolerite

Naddle

S. John's

Shoul-thwaite

Ullswater

limestone Skiddaw Slates

limestone

Mosedale

Crummock Water

Derwent Water

Thirlmere

Boredale

Fusedale

Howe Grain

Ennerdale Water

Butter-mere

Seathwaite

Rosthwaite

Helvellyn △

Grisedale

Goldrill

Hawes Water

granophyre

Pillar △

Langstrath

Brothers Water

High Street △

Swindale

54° 30'

Wast Water

Scafell Pikes △

Langdale

Grasmere

Rydal Water

Trout Beck

Kent Mere

Longsleddale

Bannisdale

Irt

Elter Water

granite

Little Langdale

Duddon

Mite

Esk

Coniston Old Man △

Coniston Water

Grisedale

Torver

Esthwaite Water

Windermere

Winster

limestone

Lat 54° 20' N

limestone

old sea shore

river capture?

former outlet?

Although the rocks which cradle the Lakes are ancient in British geological terms, the Ice Ages of the last million years have dramatically sculpted the land-forms we see today. Moraines deposited 10,000 years ago dammed many sheets of water. Sedimentation has since reduced their number and shrunk the surviving lakes and tarns. Lake District geology is a complex subject requiring study of specialist literature and maps plus fieldwork to appreciate the formation and structure of the Cumbrian Fells and their littoral.

KEY   stratigraphical order

FORMER LAKE / LAKE AREA
PRESENT EXTENT OF LAKE
SILURIAN SEDIMENTARY ROCK
CONISTON LIMESTONE SERIES
VOLCANIC INTRUSION
BORROWDALE VOLCANIC GROUP
SKIDDAW SLATES

{ based purely on the author's conjecture:-
{ these areas revert to "lakes" after heavy rain!
Thirlmere and Hawes Water's pre-reservoir extents are shown
Mud, silt, grit & fossils laid in shallow seas 410-440 million years ago
Fossil-rich shales, mudstones laid in warm shallow seas 440 m.y.a.
see map - these lavas welled up from magma deep in the earth
Complex slates, lavas. & ashes from submarine volcanoes 450 m.y.a.
Our oldest rocks, mud, shale, slate, grit & flags 500 m.y.

RIVERS AND STREAMS

Italics = outflow ► = Stream continues to next entry.
Where variations occur Ordnance Survey names have been adopted for this list.

NAME	Lake & CHART
Aik Beck	Ul IV-e
Aira Beck	Ul II-w
Appletree Syke	Es
Barrow Beck	De II-n
Beck Leven	Co III
Beckstones Gill	Ba II-s/III-n
Beck Wythop	Ba II-n
Belle Grange Beck	Wi VI-w
Ben Gill	En I-w
Birkfell Slack	Ul II-w&e
Black Beck	Wi III/IV
Black Beck	Es
Black Beck	Co II
Black Beck	Co IV
Black Pots	En I-w
Blake Beck	Wi VII-w
Bleak Beck	Wi VI-e
Blelham Beck	Wi VI-w/VII-w
Boon Beck	Co I
Boredale Beck	Ul IV-w (inset)
Bowder Beck	Bu
Bracken Burn	De II-n
Brathay ►	El
Brathay ►	El
Brathay	Wi VII-w
Brockle Beck	De I-s
Burrow Beck	Wi II/III
Buttermere Dubs	Cr II
Buttermere Dubs	Bu/Cr
Canker Beck	Es
Cat Gill	De I-s/II-n
Cat Gill	De II-n
Caws Beck	Co I
Chapel Beck	Ba I-n
Chapel Beck	Ba III-n
Char Dub	En II
Church Beck	Co IV
Cinderdale Beck	Cr I/II
Coal Beck	Ba I-n
Cocker	Cr I
Collierhag Beck	Ul II-e
Comb Beck	Bu
Comb Gill	De II-s
Comb Gill	Th III
Copplebarrow Beck	Wi II
Countess Beck	Wa I-w
Cow Close Gill	Co III
Crabtree Beck	Lo

NAME	Lake & CHART
Cragsteads Gill	Th III
Crake	Co I
Cunsey Beck ►	Es
Cunsey Beck	Wi IV
Derwent ►	De II-s
Derwent ►	De I-n
Derwent ►	Ba II-s/III-n&s
Derwent	Ba I-n
Dob Gill	Th III
Dowthwaite Gill	Th I
Dub Beck ►	Lo
Dub Beck	Lo
Dubwath Beck	Ba I-n
Dunn(e)y Beck	Gr/Ry
Eamont	Ul IV-e
Ehen	En I-w
Elder Beck	Ul IV-e
Ellers Beck	De II-s
Esthwaite Hall Beck	Es
Far Ruddy Beck	Cr II/Bu
Far Swan Beck	Ul II-w
Fisher Beck	Wi VII-e
Fisher Gill	Th I/II
Fisherplace Gill	Th I
Fusedale Beck	Ul III-e
Gatescarthdale Beck	Bu
Gatescarth Beck	Ha III
Gill Beck	Wi II/III
Gill Beck	En I-w
Gill Head Beck	Wi III
Glencoyne Beck	Ul II-w
Glenridding Beck	Ul I
Goat Gill	Wa II-w
Goldrill Beck ►	Br
Goldrill Beck	Ul I
Great Hall Gill	Wa I-w
Great Langdale Beck	El
Greenholme Beck	Co I
Greta	De I-n
Grisedale Beck	Ul I
Groove Gill	Wa II-e
Groovegill Beck	Ul II-w
Guerness Gill	Ha II
Hagg Sike	Cr II-e
Hallgarth Beck	Ba III-n&s
Halls Beck	Ba I-n
Hartley Beck	Bu
Hassnesshow Beck	Bu

Hause Gill	Th II/III		Pencillmill Beck	Ul IV-w
Hayeswater Gill	Br		Podnet Beck	Ha II
Helvellyn Gill	Th I/II		Pooley Beck	Ba I-n
Hill Gill	Co II		Pow Beck	Ba IIIn&s
Hoathwaite Beck	Co III		Pull Beck	Wi VII-w
Hoghouse Beck	Wi VI-w/VII-w		Puttsgill Sike	Ha II
Hol Beck	Wi VII-e			
Holme Beck	Lo		Raise Beck	Th III
Hollow Beck	Wi V-n		Rake Beck	En I-e
Hollow Gill	Wa II-e		Ramps Beck	Ul IV-e
Hop Gill	Ha III		Randale Beck	Ha III
Hostel Beck	Es		Rannerdale Beck	Cr I/II
How Beck	Es		Red Beck	En I-e
Howegrain Beck	Ul IV-w(inset)		Red Gill	Cr I
			Riggingdale Beck	Ha III
Irt	Wa I-w		*Rothay* ►	Gr
			Rothay ►	Gr
Kirkstone Beck	Br		Rothay ►	Ry
			Rothay ►	Ry
Ladknott Gill	Th I		Rothay	Wi VII-w
Lair Beck	Ba III-s		Rothery Sike	En I-w
Launchy Gill	Th II			
Leven	Wi I		Sail Beck	Cr II/Bu
Laythwaite Sike	Ha II		*Saint John's Beck*	Th I
Lingmell Beck	Wa II-e		Sandwick Beck	Ul III-w/IV-w
Lingmell Gill	Wa II-e		Scale Beck	Cr II
Liza	En II		Scale Beck	Ba III-n
			School Beck	Co IV
Mardale Beck ►	Ha III		Selside Beck	Co I/II
Mardale Beck	Ha I		Skill Beck	Ba II-n
Measand Beck	Ha II		Smithy Beck	Wa I-w/II-w
Middlesteads Gill	Th I/II		Smithy Beck	En I-w/II
Middle Swan Beck	Ul II-w		Smooth Beck	Es
Mill Beck	Wi V-n		Sourmilk Gill	Bu
Mill Beck	Cr II/Bu		Stanah Gill	Th I
Mill Beck	Ba III-n		Straighthead Gill	Wa II-e
Miller Beck	Wi I		Swarthbeck Gill	Ul III-e
Mill Gill	Th I			
Mines Gill	Th II/III		Thrang Gill	Th I
Moor Gill	Co III		Torver Beck	Co II
Mosedale Beck	Wa II-e		Trout Beck	Wi VI-e
Mosedale Beck	Lo			
Mossydale Beck	Ul I		Warnscale Beck	Bu
			Watendlath Beck	De II-s
Naddle Beck	Ha I		Wath Beck	Ba III-n
Near Ruddy Gill	Bu		Whelpside Gill	Th III
Near Swan Beck	Ul II-w		Whelter Beck	Ha II/III
Nether Beck	Wa II-w		Wilfin Beck	Wi IV
Newlands Beck	Ba II-s/III-n&s		Withe Sike	De II-n
Nook Sike	Ha II		Woundell Beck	En II
			Wray Gill	Gr
Over Beck	Wa II-w		Wyke Gill	Gr
			Wynlass Beck	Wi V-n/VI-e
Park Beck ►	Lo		Wyth Burn	Th III
Park Beck	Cr I			
Parkhouse Gill	Ul II-w		Yewdale Beck	Co IV

MINOR TARNS AND RIVER FEATURES *(italics)*

Name	CHART		
Allan Tarn	Co I	*Joe Barron's Pool*	De I-n
Bottom Clay Pool	Ba III-n	*King's Wheel*	Wi VII-w
Brathay Hall Tarn	Wi VII-w	*Landing Hole*	Wi I
Bridges Hole	Ba II-n	*Leathside Dub*	De II-s
Cannon Dub	De II-s	*Low Lonning Pool*	Ba III-s
Dick Tyson Is	De I-n	Out Dubs Tarn	Es
Fitts Turnhole	De II-s	*Pipe End Pool*	Ba III-s
Gill Dubs	Ha I	Priest Pot	Es
How Grassings Pool	Ba III-s	*Shilton Pool*	De I-n
Ingshead Hole	De II-s	*Stocks Bridge Pool*	Ba III-n
		Top Clay Pool	Ba III-n

HEADLANDS AND BAYS *(italics)*

Name	CHART		
Abbot's Bay	De II-n	*Church Bay*	Ba II-n
Aira Point	Ul II-w	*Cabin, The*	Co II/III
Anglers' Crag	En I-w	*Calfclose Bay*	De I-s
Anna's Nab	Co I	Cannon Crag	Wi IV
Ash Landing	Wi IV	*Castle Bay*	Wi VI-w
		Castlehows Point	Ul IV-w
Banks Point	Ba I-n	Clark's Loup	Th II
Barrow Bay	De II-n	*Clay or Tadpole Dub*	En I-e
Barrow Point	De II-n	Coatlap Point	Wi V-s
Bass Crag	Co I	Cock Point	Co III
Bass Crag	Co II	Cockshott Point	Wi V-s
Bass Howe	Wi V-n	*Copperheap Bay*	De I-s
Belle Grange Bay	Wi V-n/VI-w	*Cunsey Bay*	Wi IV
Bellman's Hole	Co II		
Birk Ness	Bu-e	*Derwent Bay*	De I-s
Black Hole	Wi II	*Devil's Chimney*	Ul I
Black Rock	Th II	Dog Nab	Wi III
Blackstock Point	Ba II-s	*Dove Nest Bay*	Wi VII-e
Blackwell Bay	Wi IV		
Blakeholme Nab	Wi II	Ees	Es-s
Blea Brows	Co I	*Ees Wyke*	Es-s
Blea Wick	Ul I	Elter Holme	Es-s
Boscombe Rigg	Ul II-e	Ewe Crag	Ul II-w/e
Bow Ness	En I-e		
Bow Ness	Ba II-n	Ferry Nab	Wi IV/V-s
Bowness Bay	Wi V-s	Friar's Crag	De I-s
Bowness Bay	Ba I-s/II-n		
Brandlehow Bay	De II-n	*Gale Bay*	Ul IV-e
Brandlehow Point	De II-n	*Galemire Bay*	De I-n
Brathay Bay	Wi VII-w	Gale Naze Crag	Wi VII-w
Brathay Neck	Wi VII-w	Geordie's Crag	Ul III-w
Brathay Rocks	Wi VII-w	*Gowbarrow Bay*	Ul III-w
Broad Ness	Ba I-s/II-n	*Great Bay*	De II-s
Brock Crag	Wi VII-w	*Green Naze Wyke*	Wi IV
Broomhill Point	De I-s	*Grubbins Point, The*	Wi III
		Grub Hole	Es-n

Hammer Hole	Wi III		Rawlinson Nab	Wi III
Harlies Crag	Wi II		*Rayrigg Wyke*	Wi V-n
Hause Point	Cr II-w		Red Nab	Wi VI-w
Hause Point	Th II/III		Red Ness	Ba II-s/III-n
High Peel Near	Co II		Robin Hood's Seat	En I-w
High Wray Bay	Wi VI-w		*Riddings Bay*	Wi I
Hodgson Hill	Ul IV-e		Rigg, The	Ha III
Holbeck Point	Wi VII-e		Ringing Crag	Wi I/II
Houseboat Bay	Wi IV		*Robin Wyke*	Es-s
Howtown Wyke	Ul III-e			
Hursthole Point	Ba II-s		Sand Beds	Wi VI-w
			Sand Wick	Ul III-w
Isthmus Bay	De I-n		*Sandy Wyke*	Wi VII-w
			Scar Ness	Ba I-s
Jemmy Crag	Wi IV		*Scarness Bay*	Ba I-s
			Sharrow Bay	Ul III-e
Kailpot Bay	Ul III-w		*Silver Bay*	Ul I/II-w
Kailpot Crag	Ul III-w		Silver Point	Ul I/II-w
Kitchen Bay	De I-s		Skelly Nab	Ul III-w
			Slape Scar	Wi V-n
Lands Point	Co IV		*Sourpool Wyke*	Wi IV/V-s
Lazy Bay	Wi III		Spit, The	Ul I
Lily Bay	Wi VII-w		Stewardson's Nab	Wi III
Long Tongue	Wi II		Storrs Temple	Wi IV
Low Grounds Point	Wi VII-w		*Strandshag Bay*	De I-s
Low Ling Crag	Cr II-w		Strickland Ees	Es-s
Low Peel Near	Co I/II		*Swan Nest*	Wi VI-e
Low Wray Bay	Wi VI-w/VII-w		*Swan's Nest*	Lo
			Swarthbeck Point	Ul III-e
Millerground Bay	Wi V-n/VI-e			
Mitchell Wyke	Wi IV/V-s		*Tablerock Bay*	Ul III-w
Montague Wyke	Co II		*Tadpole or Clay Dub*	En I-e
Mossydale Bay	Ul I		*Ten Tree Bay*	Es-s
Myrtle Bay	De II-s		*Thwaitehill Bay*	Ul III-e
			Thwaitehill Neb	Ul III-e
Nab	Es-n			
Nab, The	El		*Victoria Bay*	De II-n
Nether How	Cr II-w			
			Watbarrow Point	Wi VI-w
Oldchurch Bay	Ul III-e		*Water End*	Co I
Otterbield Bay	De I-s/II-n		*Water Foot*	Ul IV-e
Oxenhouse Bay	Co II		*Water Head*	Co IV
			Waterhead Bay	Wi VII-w
Park Nab	Co I		*Weather Bay*	Es-s
Park Neb	De II-s		*White Cross Bay*	Wi VI-e
Parsonage Bay	Wi V-s		*Withesike Bay*	De II-n
Peartree Point	Wi II		Woodclose Point	Wi VI-w
Peel Wyke	Ba I-s		Wray Crag	Wi VI-w/VII-w
Pinstones Point	Wi VI-w		*Wyke, The*	Gr
Pull Wyke	Wi VII-w			
Purse Point	Ul I		Yew How	Th II

THE ISLANDS

Where alternatives occur Ordnance Survey names have been adopted for this list.
x = no landing. *Italics* = rocks (≋ = submerged or awash).

Island or *Rock*	CHART		Island or *Rock*	CHART
Bass Rock	Wi V-n/VI-w		*Lingy Holme*	Ul I
Bee Holme x	Wi VII-w		*Lingy Stone*	Ry
Belle Isle x	Wi V-s		*Little Island* x	Ry
Black Crag	Ry		*Little Isle*	En I-w
Blake Holme	Wi II		Lord's Island x	De I-s
Bull Head ≋	Wi IV			
			Maiden Holme	Wi IV/V-s
Calf Rock	Co II		*Matson Shoal* ≋	Wi IV
Carlew Crag ≋	Wi IV		*Midwater Shoals* ≋	Wi IV
Cherry Holme	Ul I		*Mossy Stone*	Wi VI-w
Chicken Rock ≋	Wi IV/V-s			
Costrell Rocks	Wi II		Nab Island x	El
Crow Holme	Wi IV/V-s		Norfolk Island x o	Ul I/II-w
Crag Holme	Wi III			
Curlew Crag	Wi V-s		Oak Isle x	Co I
			Otterbield Island	De I-s/II-n
Deergarth How x	Th II		Otter Island	De II-n
Derwent Island x	De I-n/s		*Oven Bottom* ≋	Wi IV
Ecclerigg Crag	Wi VI-w		Park Neb	De II-s
Epley Point	Wi VI-w		Peel Island	Co I
			Peely Slapehold ≋	Ul III-e
Fir Holme x	Wi V-s			
Fir Island x	Co III		Ramp Holme	Wi IV
			Ramps Holme	De I-s
Grass Holme	Wi III		*Robin Shoals* ≋	Es
Green Holme	Ry		Rough Holme x	Wi V-n
Green Tuft ≋	Wi VII-w			
			Saint Herbert's Island	De I-s
Harrop Rocks	Wi II/III		*Sandy Nab* ≋	Wi IV
Hartley Wife	Wi V-s		Scale Island	Cr II-w
Hawes Holme	Wi V-s		*Scarf Stones* ≋	De I-s/II-n
Hawes How x	Th II		*Seamew Crag*	Wi VII-w
Hen Rock ≋	Wi IV/V-s		Silver Holme	Wi II/III
Hen Holme x	Wi V-n		*Skirtful Crags* ≋	Wi II
Heron Isle x	Ry		Stake Holme x	Wi V-s
Holme Crag	Wi VII-w			
Holme Islands	Cr II-w		The Island x	Gr
			Thompson's Holme	Wi V-s
Iron Stone	Cr II-w		Thrang Crag x	Ry
			Tuft Crag ≋	Wi V-n
Kid Haw x	Wi I			
			Wall Holme	Ul I
Lady Holme x	Wi V-n		Woodhouse Island	Cr II-w
Lilies of the Valley	Wi V-s		Wood Howe x	Ha III
Ling Holme	Wi IV		*White Cross*	Wi VI-e

96

ADMINISTRATIVE BOUNDARIES
Lake Parishes and District Councils

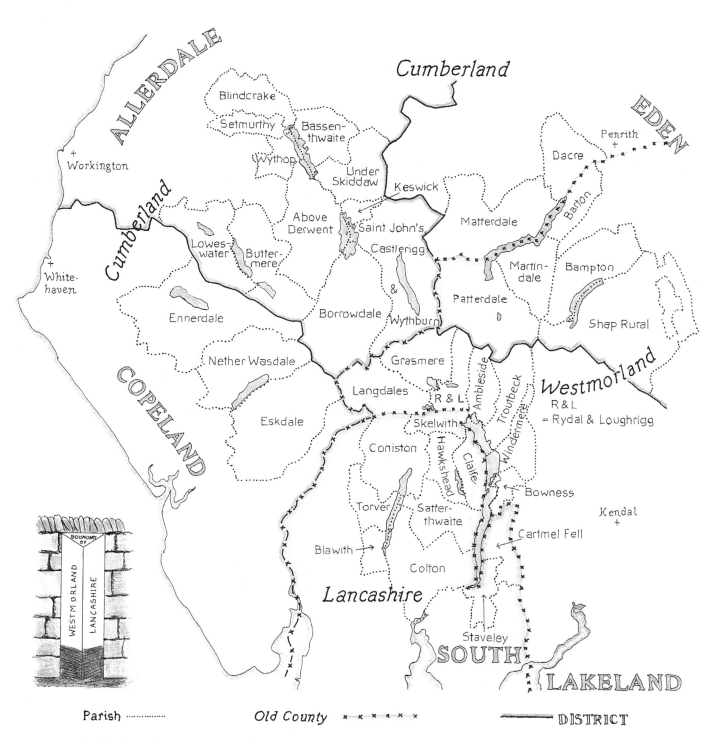

Parish ············· Old County ×–×–×–×–×–× ——— DISTRICT

Parish Boundaries appear on Ordnance Survey Outdoor Leisure Maps (see pg 15). Generally they remained unaffected by the local government re-organisation of 1974. District Councils are components of CUMBRIA COUNTY COUNCIL which replaced the historical Lake Counties. All the lakes are situated within the NATIONAL PARK boundary which is not included on this diagram.

A SELECT BIBLIOGRAPHY

The Lake District must be the most widely documented area of comparable size in the world. Every aspect has been examined in the minutest detail by a variety of experts and amateurs during the last two centuries. Bookshops-full are always in print, such is the popularity of The Lakes with both bookworm and lover of the outdoors. In producing yet another tome to add to this increasing pile of paper I derived inspiration, advice and the most interesting and relevant information from the following:

THE LAKE COUNTIES
W. G. Collingwood
Revised by William Rollinson, London 1988

THE LAKES
W. Heaton Cooper
Frank Peters Publishing, Kendal 1987

OUTWARD BOUND CANOEING & SAILING HANDBOOKS
Maggie Annat & Martin Balcombe
Ward Lock, London 1995

RIVERS OF CUMBRIA: A CANOEIST'S GUIDE
Mike Hayward
Cordee, Leicester 1992

THE PLACE NAMES OF CUMBRIA
Joan Lee
Cumbria Heritage Services, Carlisle 1998

LAKE DISTRICT ANGLERS' GUIDE
Laurence Tetley
Cicerone Press, Milnthorpe 1999

PICTORIAL GUIDES TO THE LAKELAND FELLS (8 Vols)
A. Wainwright
Michael Joseph.

THE CANOEIST
Monthly magazine covering every discipline of the sport/pastime.
4 Sinodum Row, Appleford, Oxon OX14 4PE

CUMBRIA
For fifty years, an obligatory monthly read for anyone with an intrest in, or regard for, the Lake District and surroundings. Modest in price and approach, Cumbria maintains a well-informed and intimate rapport with the folk who contribute to the welfare of residents or visitors, maintain the landscape of the County and promote outdoor and cultural events.
Dalesman Publishing Co Ltd, Skipton.

GETTING AROUND CUMBRIA
Time-tables for Boats, Buses and Trains.
Published twice a year and available from Information Centres.
Cumbria County Council and public service operators.

A WALK AROUND THE LAKES
Hunter Davies
Weidenfeld and Nicolson 1979

USEFUL ADDRESSES

TOURIST INFORMATION OFFICES (◑ = seasonal opening)

LAKE	LOCATION	telephone	authority
Windermere	Bowness-on-W ◑	015394 42895	National Park
	Brockhole Visitor Cen ◑	015394 46601	National Park
	Fell Foot ◑	015395 31273	National Trust
	Waterhead ◑	015394 32729	National Park
	Windermere town	01539 446499	Tourist Board
Grasmere	Grasmere village ◑	015394 35245	National Park
Rydal Water & Elter Water	Ambleside	015394 32582	Tourist Board
Esthwaite Water	Hawkshead ◑	015394 36525	National Park
Coniston Water	Coniston village ◑	015394 41533	National Park
Wast Water & Ennerdale Water	Egremont	01946 820693	Tourist Board
Lowes Wr, Crummock Wr & Buttermere	Cockermouth	01900 822634	Tourist Board
Derwent Water, Bassenthwaite Lake & Thirlmere Reservoir	Keswick (Moot Hall)	017687 72645	N P & T B
	" (Discovery Cen)	017687 72803	National Park
	" (Lakeside) ◑	017687 73780	National Trust
Ullswater & Brothers Water	Glenridding ◑	017684 82414	National Park
	Pooley Bridge ◑	017684 86530	National Park
Haweswater Reservoir	Penrith	01768 867466	Tourist Board
	Bampton Post Office	01931 713351	National Park

LAKE DISTRICT NATIONAL PARK AUTHORITY
National Park Office, Murley Moss, Oxenholme Road, KENDAL, Cumbria LA9 7RL
tel 01539 724555
General Enquiries and Windermere Boat Registration.

THE NATIONAL TRUST
North West Regional Office, The Hollens, Grasmere, AMBLESIDE, Cumbria LA11 9QZ
tel 0870 609 5 391

THE BRITISH CANOE UNION
John Dudderidge House, Adbolton Lane, West Bridgford, NOTTINGHAM NG2 5AS
tel 0115 9821100

THE RAMBLERS' ASSOCIATION
Camelford House, 87-89 Albert Embankment, LONDON SE1 7BR
tel 020 7339 8500

ROYAL YACHTING ASSOCIATION
RYA House, Romsey Road, EASTLEIGH, Hants SO50 9YA
tel 01703 629962

YOUTH HOSTELS ASSOCIATION
Trevelyan House, Dimple Road, MATLOCK, Derbys DE4 3YH
tel 0870 770 8868

TRAVELINE CUMBRIA
up-to-date information about road, rail and lake transport
tel 0870 608 2 608

EPILOGUE

When, in late 1997, we began a systematic exploration of each lake, people would query the availability of a guidebook for boat-users. Although leaflets issued by the National Trust and Park Authority provided fragmentary information, chiefly related to the important issue of access, it seemed no book - or at least a practical guide- devoted to the very features which give this famous region its essential character, was in print. On the maps lots of rocks, islets, reeds and shingle were omitted and new lakeside paths (indicated as permitted or rights-of-way) not surveyed.

By the following spring I found employment annotating maps and recording observations during our excursions. Jenny became used to clinging on or tying-up to mid-water obstructions while positions were fixed. The "chore" of surveying shore-walks led to the discovery of unexpectedly entertaining rambles. Acclaim is due those workers who have constructed these paths. Folk encountered on our rounds - proprietors and locals, as well as walkers and canoeists - took an encouraging interest. On 14th June 2000 my field-book slipped from the car's roof when leaving Ennerdale. Thank You to the kind unknown who posted it home. And aye, who quipped "Oh - a sort of Wet Wainwright!"? We trust the results come some way towards expectations.

While we were working I reckon a total 247 miles (397 kilometres) of roads and footways were recorded. Of these, 159 miles (256 kilometres) are necessary to repeat the walking circuits of all seventeen lakes. Jenny usually accompanied me on these landward surveys. Now and again a bicycle was employed, at least as a means of return (buses were rarely useful). Together we paddled or rowed along the 124 miles (200 kilometres) of shoreline on those waters available for such activities - and then some more- either to return to our put-in or re-visit shorelines where lake levels were subject to significant variation. The remaining "no-go" 15 miles (26 kilometres) had to be observed from varied viewpoints to complete the fieldwork. Distances around individual lakes appear on the "Around the Shores" or "On the Water" summary maps in the introductory pages.

Designing and formatting the Charts proved an absorbing exercise. Including all the features with some consistency was gained by varied means. Apart from filling in the corners, the notes were, hopefully, introduced to provide background for newcomers to Lakeland. Might their brevity and serendipity encourage further study and interest in the Ecology, History and Topography of the District? There is no shortage of published material. A broad range of well-written, definitive accounts and guides may be chosen from the shelves of discerning booksellers. However a dwindling number of specialist subjects such as Notable Houses, Steamers or Lake Transport remain ripe for investigation.

Readers requiring an introduction to any water-based recreation should discover this region can serve them well. Outdoor Centres organised by expert individuals, Local Authorities or Youth Organisations as well as Sailing and Canoe Clubs are established on the major lakes.

Algal blooms have been a recent problem. They are manifested in greenish, soupy mists pervading the waters during the summer months. Over-rich discharges and de-oxygenisation create conditions which may render swimming unsafe in lakes bordered by agricultural land and urban areas.

We remembered Christopher North's favourite time to visit the Lakes lasted from the first of January until the thirty-first of December. Adhering to this premise we experienced their variety of symphonic mood. Windermere evoked Handelian Water Music, Coniston Water - Elgarian Affection, Wast Water - Sibelian Tone Poem, Derwent Water - Beethovenian Overture, Ullswater - Wagnerian Drama.

Even as its nautical conclusion is drawn below, events might render detail in this book out-of-date. Intended as an objective survey, it is offered as a record of The Lakes at the Dawn of the Third Millennium......

December 2000   John Wilson Parker

LEGEND

N.B. Excepting rock and water, **colour** denotes public access or facilities. See p 17

public ROAD: ⟨symbol⟩ TRACK: ⟨symbol⟩   PARKING: unrestricted ⟨symbol⟩

PATH: along private road ⟨symbol⟩ track ⟨symbol⟩   PARKING: subject to charge ⟨symbol⟩

surfaced ⟨symbol⟩ trodden ⟨symbol⟩ indistinct ⟨symbol⟩   BUS service 🚌   seasonal facility ◑

steps ⟨symbol⟩ gate ⟨symbol⟩ stile ⟨symbol⟩

wall ⟨symbol⟩ hedge ⟨symbol⟩ fence ⟨symbol⟩   picnic site ⟨symbol⟩   play area K

                                                    camping ⟨symbol⟩   tourers ⟨symbol⟩

PASSENGER steamer, ⟨symbol⟩ launch ⟨symbol⟩   lawn, parkland ⟨symbol⟩   National Trust land ⟨symbol⟩

canoe "PUT-IN": free ⟨symbol⟩ fee ⟨symbol⟩   National Park ⟨symbol⟩   Forest Enterprise ⟨symbol⟩

LAUNCHING for sailing craft ⟨symbol⟩   building with PUBLIC FACILITIES ⟨symbol⟩

stone embankment, quay ⟨symbol⟩   private house, outbuilding, boat house ⟨symbol⟩

wooden landing stage ⟨symbol⟩   toilets W C   tourist info. office ⟨symbol⟩

fixed danger marker ⟨symbol⟩ life-belt O   post office ✉   telephone kiosk × ☎

woodland ⟨symbol⟩ fir ⟨symbol⟩ coppice ⟨symbol⟩   FOOD: eat "in" or "out"

azalea, etc ⟨symbol⟩ gorse ⟨symbol⟩ bracken etc ⟨symbol⟩   restaurant ⟨symbol⟩   café,teas ⟨symbol⟩ pub, bar ⟨symbol⟩

heath ⟨symbol⟩ cliff & rock ⟨symbol⟩ scree ⟨symbol⟩   take-away ⟨symbol⟩   shop ⟨symbol⟩ D.I.Y. ⟨symbol⟩

WATER ⟨symbol⟩ stream ⟨symbol⟩ marsh ⟨symbol⟩

reeds ⟨symbol⟩ rocks ⟨symbol⟩ shingle ⟨symbol⟩   BOAT HIRE: motor ⟨symbol⟩

DON'T DISTURB! take care of the countryside   sailing ⟨symbol⟩   rowing X

wildfowl ⟨symbol⟩ pasture ⟨symbol⟩ crops ⟨symbol⟩   kayak ⟨symbol⟩   Canadian canoe ⟨symbol⟩

SCALES

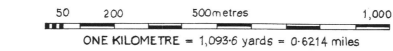

50   200   500 metres   1,000

ONE KILOMETRE = 1,093·6 yards = 0·6214 miles

100 220 yards   3 furlongs 880 yards   6 furlongs   1,760 yds

ONE MILE = 1,609·34 metres or 1·609 kilometres = 5,280 feet = 63,360 inches

608 feet 405 yds, 1ft   ½ nautical ml   800 fathoms   100 cables

OLD NAUTICAL MILE = 1,853·18 metres = 1 mile, 266 yards, 2 feet = 6,080 feet = 100 cables

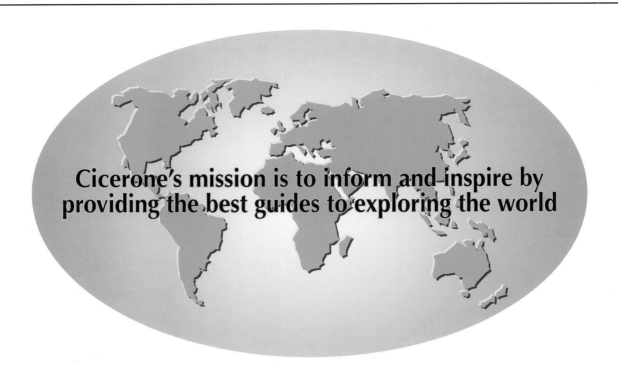

Cicerone's mission is to inform and inspire by providing the best guides to exploring the world

Since its foundation over 30 years ago, Cicerone has specialised in publishing guidebooks and has built a reputation for quality and reliability. It now publishes nearly 300 guides to the major destinations for outdoor enthusiasts, including Europe, UK and the rest of the world.

Written by leading and committed specialists, Cicerone guides are recognised as the most authoritative. They are full of information, maps and illustrations so that the user can plan and complete a successful and safe trip or expedition – be it a long face climb, a walk over Lakeland fells, an alpine traverse, a Himalayan trek or a ramble in the countryside.

With a thorough introduction to assist planning, clear diagrams, maps and colour photographs to illustrate the terrain and route, and accurate and detailed text, Cicerone guides are designed for ease of use and access to the information.

If the facts on the ground change, or there is any aspect of a guide that you think we can improve, we are always delighted to hear from you.

Cicerone Press
2 Police Square Milnthorpe Cumbria LA7 7PY
Tel:01539 562 069   Fax:01539 563 417
e-mail:info@cicerone.co.uk   web:www.cicerone.co.uk

CICERONE